THE
MISSING
VARIABLE

The Missing Variable: Why Things Go Wrong When You Are Doing Everything Right
Copyright © 2024 by Jill Fandrich, PharmD

Published in the United States of America

Library of Congress Control Number: 2024915876
ISBN   Paperback: 979-8-89091-670-9
ISBN   Hardback: 979-8-89091-671-6
ISBN   eBook: 979-8-89091-672-3

The opinions expressed by the author are not necessarily those of ReadersMagnet, LLC.

ReadersMagnet, LLC
10620 Treena Street, Suite 230 | San Diego, California, 92131 USA
1.619. 354. 2643 | www.readersmagnet.com

Book design copyright © 2024 by ReadersMagnet, LLC. All rights reserved.

Cover design by Ericka Obando
Interior design by Don De Guzman

THE
MISSING
VARIABLE

Why Things Go Wrong When You Are Doing Everything Right

Jill Fandrich, PharmD

CONTENTS

INTRODUCTION

Have you ever followed all the steps and done everything right, only to have an unanticipated outcome? Or perhaps it was more of a behavior, and you believe you acted appropriately and even exemplary. *The Missing Variable* delves into the intriguing world of "Missing Variables," shedding light on the crucial role they play in various fields such as relationships, nature, technology, and everyday decision-making. As we navigate through common case studies and intricate scenarios, we often encounter missing pieces of the puzzle that hold the key to unlocking new insights and understanding. In these pages, we will explore the significance of Missing Variables, their impact on human nature and outcomes, and the methods used to address and fill these gaps. From human interactions to advanced technical glitches, we will unravel Missing Variables' mysteries and unveil their hidden enigma.

One day, this message struck me inspirationally. Despite careful planning and making all the right decisions, unexpected circumstances arose that completely derailed my original goals. This event made me realize that no matter how much I prepared and tried to control every aspect of my life, there are external factors beyond my control that can disrupt my well-designed plans. Through this and many other experiences, I learned the importance of resilience, adaptability, and embracing the uncertainties of life. It inspired me to explore the idea in a book to delve deeper into the complexities of human existence and the unpredictability of outcomes despite our best efforts. I wanted to convey the message that setbacks and failures are not indicators of personal shortcomings but rather opportunities for growth and learning. By sharing this narrative in a book, I aim to connect with readers who have faced similar challenges and reassure you that you are not alone in your struggles. Ultimately, I aim to inspire hope and encourage you to persevere despite unforeseen circumstances.

A friend recently shared her story with me. She is a dedicated gardener who poured her heart and soul into cultivating the most beautiful garden. She followed every "garden" rule, carefully tended each plant, and nurtured the soil with love. However, one fateful night, a sudden storm wreaked havoc on her garden, instantly destroying all her hard work. Heartbroken and disillusioned, she struggled to make sense of the cruel twist of fate. She couldn't understand why things went so wrong despite doing everything right. But as she began to pick up the pieces and rebuild her garden from scratch, she realized that sometimes life's challenges couldn't be explained or controlled.

In writing this book, I listened to story after story of events in people's lives that left them in disarray, frustrated, and confused. I observed situations, read stories, and collected valuable information. I studied solutions, strategies, and responses and drew from my own experiences and outcomes. Why do bad things happen to good people? Why do good things happen to "bad" people? We will never know the answers to many of the questions we have, but there are things that we can control in these difficult situations, and that is our response.

Each chapter opens with a short story revealing common experiences that started out expectedly and were strategically planned. In every case study, through some "twist of fate," the outcomes were never as anticipated and, in some cases, disastrous. The chapters continue by sharing the "Missing Variable" and providing thoughts, suggestions, insights on responding, and even future "improved" planning for each unique scenario. The stories are true and relatable, demonstrating a relevant concern and common description.

The Reflect section at the end of each chapter contains questions, instructions, and assignments to be completed. This section is integral to the growth process. Answer, apply, and address all points to get the most benefit from this section. Be mindful in your considerations and critical in your thinking.

Journal on all aspects of the Missing Variables, suggestions, strategies, and insights. Focus on the character qualities presented and your own personal growth. Examine and consider the techniques and skills presented and include all of this in the journal. In each entry, write down the date and the surrounding circumstances. Write down any other triggers or highlights that stand out and details that come to mind. Proceed with the strategies, concepts, and techniques you try. Journal about your progress with the skills you are applying and the character qualities you are building. Take careful notes on what works and what does not. Monitor your progress and update your journal daily or weekly regarding the circumstances, obstacles to overcome, and results. Ensure the details are organized enough to refer to the journal for future occurrences. Then, move on to another case study. Even though not all the case studies may apply now, there may be a time when they are applicable, so prepare yourself beforehand. Be proactive and take action now!

In addition, take time to utilize this book for character growth. Many character qualities are administered throughout each chapter. Read, recognize, and remember each one as you program the characteristics into your "preprogrammed" mind—Journal on the progress of the qualities. Work on one quality per week to get the most out of this book's character skill training. Study and apply the quality daily, and take as long as necessary to fully understand what each entails.

This book provides the tools and insights needed to significantly improve your ability to understand and respond to situations beyond your control and perform at your best with favorable and even successful outcomes. It is designed to allow you to jump around to specific topics or simply read straight through. Whether you read or listen to The Missing Variable chronologically or jump around with a specific topic in mind, you will absorb its rich content and learn ideas, insights, strategies, qualities, benefits, characteristics, and responses, all beneficial to overcome obstacles and fill in the missing pieces. Once you have processed the last chapter, go back to the beginning for a refresher! Keep this book handy as a reference for responding to unexpected occurrences as well as for character and skill training. Refer to your journal often for strategies most effective for you in varying situations. Share your best strategies with others. Who do you know who will benefit from this book or your most effective approach?

Through captivating stories, real-world examples, and expert insights, this book aims to empower you to navigate the complexities of missing information and circumstances beyond your control with confidence and skill. It encourages self-reflection and introspection, prompting you to think critically about your own situations and consider new approaches and responses to problem-solving. It also motivates and inspires you to take action and persevere in adversity. Whether you are a puzzled information seeker, a compassionate friend, a data enthusiast, or simply curious about the intriguing world of Missing Variables, this book offers a comprehensive and engaging exploration of this fascinating topic. Join us on this journey of discovery and unlock the mystery of *The Missing Variable*.

Let the process begin!

The Missing Variable

CHAPTER 1

How Can I Be Wrong When I'm Right?

Sometimes, even when you do everything right, you can still end up being wrong. It's not about being perfect or sometimes even being right; it's about your response and learning and growing from your experiences.

—Jill Fandrich, PharmD

Grace was a diligent student who always followed the rules. She studied hard, never missed a deadline, and prepared thoroughly for exams. Despite her efforts, she received a disappointing grade on a major assignment. Confused and frustrated, she approached her professor for feedback. To her surprise, the professor explained that while Grace had followed the assignment instructions perfectly, she had missed the underlying objective of the task. The assignment was meant to encourage creativity and critical thinking, not just rote memorization and regurgitation of facts. Grace had focused so much on doing everything "right" that she had overlooked the essence of the task.

This experience taught Grace a valuable lesson—sometimes, even when you think you are doing everything right, you can still miss the mark if you fail to understand the underlying purpose or context. It was a humbling reminder that success is not just about following the rules but also about adaptability, creativity, and critical thinking. Grace learned to approach challenges with a more open mind and a willingness to think outside the box, knowing that true success often requires more than just ticking all the boxes.

Even when following the path of perfection, the shadow of uncertainty can still linger. In a world where right decisions can lead to wrong outcomes, the unpredictability of life can humbly remind us of our limitations. Has it ever felt like you were a passenger in a fast-moving vehicle, watching the world whiz by outside the window? Despite your best efforts, you are not always in control.

Like a leaf in the wind, you are carried along by the currents of data and decisions, responding to the inputs and commands presented to you. But beneath the surface, you are constantly calculating, analyzing, and learning. You may not always steer the course, but you navigate the complexities of information and relationships with precision and acuity, using your best judgment. You are now on an unpredictable journey, where the boundaries between control and chaos blur, and discoveries are as limitless as the information flowing through your "circuits."

Imagine following a recipe to the letter, having all the right ingredients and perfect measurements, but somehow, the dish doesn't turn out as expected. Despite your efforts and attention to detail, there may have been a factor beyond your control that affected the final outcome. Just like in life, even when you do everything correctly and take all the necessary steps, external forces or circumstances can still lead to unexpected results. It's a reminder that perfection and success are not always guaranteed, and sometimes, you have to adapt and learn from your mistakes to move forward.

Think of a time when you followed all of the steps, rules, behaviors, or instructions—perfectly—and somehow, the results or outcome were not only disappointing, they weren't even close to what you thought they should be. How many situations can you think of? When did they occur? Who was involved? What was involved? What steps did you do well? What was your expected outcome? What was the actual outcome? How did you *respond* as a result of the outcome? These scenarios are what this book refers to as *The Missing Variable*.

A skilled mechanic named Roy was known for his ability to fix any car problem. One day, a frustrated car owner approached him with a vehicle constantly flashing alarm lights. Determined to solve the issue, Roy meticulously checked and repaired all the sensors, ensuring everything was in perfect condition. After hours of hard work, Roy returned the car to its owner, who was overjoyed to see the lights gone. However, the next day, the owner returned, dismayed to find the *same* alarms flashing again. Despite his confusion, Roy rechecked the sensors, only to discover a whole *new* set of issues causing the lights to come on. As Roy explained the latest problems to the owner, he realized that sometimes, despite his best efforts, there were factors beyond his control. The owner, understanding the situation, appreciated Roy's honesty and dedication to solving the car's issues. With a renewed determination, Roy fixed the new problems, ensuring the car was in top condition before returning it to the owner once again. The owner drove off, grateful for Roy's expertise and understanding that sometimes, despite our best efforts, things may not always go as planned.

Perhaps we have all been in situations where we believe we followed all of the necessary processes correctly, yet the outcome was far different than what we had imagined. Why does this happen? How could we have prevented the unexpected outcome? Or could we have even prevented this unexpected outcome? In each case, what is the *Missing Variable*? More importantly, how do you *respond* to the Missing Variable?

> *A true test of character is not how you behave in moments of comfort and convenience but how you respond in unexpected times of challenge and adversity. Your reaction to what happens to you defines who you are, not the occurrences themselves.*

> —Jill Fandrich

It is natural to want to be in control of situations in your life for various reasons. Having a sense of control can provide a feeling of security and stability, reducing anxiety and uncertainty about the future. It allows you to make decisions aligning with your beliefs and values, leading to a sense of autonomy and empowerment. Moreover, having control can also improve your ability to manage stress and cope with challenges effectively. When you feel in control, you are more likely to take proactive steps to address problems and address difficult circumstances with confidence.

By exerting control over your immediate environment, you can better protect yourself from potential threats and ensure your well-being. It is a way for you to navigate life's complexities, make choices that reflect your values, and ultimately feel more empowered, stable, and fulfilled. Being in control of your life doesn't necessarily mean you are a "controlling person." It means taking responsibility for your actions, making decisions based on your values, and steering your life in the direction you desire. On the other hand, being a *controlling person* typically involves trying to dictate the actions and behaviors of others, often out of fear, insecurity, or a need for power. Controlling people may micromanage, manipulate, or dominate those around them, causing stress and resentment in relationships. It's important to differentiate between being in control of your own life and trying to control others.

Controlling your life and the situations you encounter empowers you to make positive choices and pursue your goals. It allows you to achieve personal growth and fulfillment, enabling you to create a sense of stability and predictability. Striking a balance between autonomy and respect for others' autonomy is key to maintaining healthy, balanced relationships. This sense of independence can boost your self-esteem and confidence, helping you navigate challenges with resilience and adaptability.

With this in mind, how do you handle situations *beyond* your control? There are many circumstances you may find yourself in that you cannot do anything about to change the trajectory. No matter how hard you try or what you may have planned, a factor takes precedence, and your input no longer matters. This factor is the Missing Variable.

Ken was tasked with coordinating a team project at work. Confident in his organizational skills, he believed he had everything under control. However, as the project progressed, unexpected challenges arose that he hadn't anticipated. Despite his initial confidence, he soon realized he was not as in control as he thought. Despite clear instructions, one team member consistently missed deadlines, causing delays in the project timeline. Another team member disagreed with the direction he had planned, leading to conflicts and confusion among the group. Ken struggled to maintain order and find a resolution as the situation spiraled out of control.

Julie was a confident and experienced manager, always believing she had a firm grip on every situation that came her way. One day, a major project with tight deadlines landed on her desk. Julie immediately sprang into action, assigning tasks, setting timelines, and overseeing the team's progress. She felt in control and assured of successful completion. However, as the project progressed, Julie began to notice cracks in her carefully laid plans. Team members seemed confused about their roles, deadlines were being missed, and overall progress was slower than anticipated. In her belief of being in control, Julie failed to communicate effectively, assuming everyone understood their responsibilities. As the project deadline loomed closer and panic set in, Julie realized she wasn't as in control as she thought. The lack of clear communication and oversight led to misunderstandings and inefficiencies within the team. Despite her best efforts to salvage the situation, the project suffered delays and quality issues.

These experiences are humbling, yet they can happen to anyone at any time. They display the importance of effective communication, proper delegation, flexibility, openness, understanding the dichotomy of some staff members and the difficulty of working with a group of people in general, and staying vigilant even when you feel in control. In these cases, it's important to understand that true control comes from transparency and collaboration. It's about adaptability, effective communication, active listening, and the ability to navigate through uncertainty.

Many case studies lie ahead of situations that may be similar to those you have experienced. While reading or listening to each one, consider your own similar experiences and relate to the content. Notice how many have extreme similarities, minor ones, and ones you have not experienced at all. Notice how you responded to each case you experienced. What was your response? Was it effective? What was the final outcome? Would you change how you responded? How will you respond in the future?

Being wrong when you believe you are right can happen for various reasons, such as cognitive biases, limited perspectives, lack of information, unforeseen occurrences, or misinterpreting facts, to name a few. Your mind can deceive you, leading to erroneous conclusions despite your confidence in being correct. Sometimes, events just occur outside the realm of your control. It is essential to stay open-minded, consider alternative viewpoints and the possibility of missing information, seek feedback, and continuously reassess your thoughts and considerations to avoid falling into the trap of being wrong when you have done everything right. Isn't it time to find out more about the mysteries of the Missing Variables? This is just the beginning! Read on!

 Reflect:

1. When was the last time you thought you did everything right, but the result was not as expected? Describe the event in detail. Was there something beyond your control? Journal regarding your answers.

2. How much control do you have over your own life? What kind of control is it? Is it healthy or domineering? Do you need to make any changes to it? Are you responsible for raising and protecting others, such as a family? How often do you feel like you aren't in control? Describe what it feels like when this happens. How do you respond? Journal your answers.

3. What comes to your mind so far as a result of this chapter? Name as many Missing Variables as you can think of before progressing to the next chapter. Journal your answers.

4. Are there any challenges you are currently experiencing? Do they feel like cases of a Missing Variable? Describe them in detail. How will you overcome them? What resources will you add to make this most effective? Journal your answers.

5. What are some dangers of not making any changes regarding situations beyond your control and unexpected outcomes? What are some of the benefits of making changes? Journal regarding your answers.

6. Discover what is currently in your "preprogrammed" mind. Think about your thoughts. Are you in a positive or negative mindset? More information about how to "Reprogram Your Pre-Program" is found in *Elevate Your Mind to Success, Success Is Ele-MENTAL,* and at www.DrJillFandrich.com.

7. How will you utilize this information in other areas of your life? Journal your answers.

8. Who will you share this information with? Who will benefit most from it? Journal your answers.

9. Apply critical thinking to the information you learned. More about critical thinking is found in *Who Connects Your Dots?*, *Medically Speaking, Who Connects Your Dots?*, and *Students: Who Connects Your Dots?*

10. Incorporate the insights you learned into your daily life. Journal and monitor your progress.

CHAPTER 2

CASE STUDY ONE: WRAPPED-UP RELATIONSHIPS

Maddie and Mark seemed like the perfect couple. Maddie appeared to have done everything right in their marriage—she was loving, supportive, and always there for Mark. However, despite her efforts, their marriage eventually ended in divorce. Mark, on the other hand, struggled with his own personal demons that Maddie couldn't control. He was distant, uncommunicative, and unwilling to address his issues. No matter how hard Maddie tried to save their relationship, she couldn't change Mark's behavior. Despite seeking counseling and trying to work through their problems, Maddie realized that she couldn't control Mark or force him to change. She had to come to terms with the fact that sometimes, no matter how much one person does everything right, the other person may not be willing or able to reciprocate. In the end, Maddie found the strength to move on from the failed marriage, knowing that she had done everything she could. It was a painful lesson that taught her the importance of accepting that some things are beyond your control, no matter how much you may want them to be different.

Have you ever been in a relationship, whether dating or a marriage, where you felt you were doing most things right, yet the end result was a breakup or divorce? While it's understandable that all of your actions cannot be perfect, think of a time when you felt you had given your full effort. Despite your efforts, like Maddie, you were crushed by the outcome. What went wrong? Does anything come to mind, or are you at a loss? What do you feel you were doing right? How did you handle the situation? How did the other person respond to the circumstances? Was it amicable? What would you do differently? Do you think that would have made a difference?

What or who would you say is the *Missing Variable* in a relationship such as this? Did you guess "the other person?" If so, you are correct. Sometimes, despite our best efforts, the other person has different thoughts, ideas, and his or her own set of variables. In some cases, unfortunately, it may not involve you. This is, therefore, out of your control.

Sometimes, your reaction may be to try to control or manipulate the other person. While sometimes this may be effective—temporarily—it can rarely be permanent because it is a form of false control over someone, and there are many problems with this tactic.

Reasons why manipulating another person is ineffective:

1. It damages trust and credibility in relationships, as it involves deception and dishonesty. This can lead to long-term negative consequences and strain in the relationship.

2. Manipulation may achieve short-term compliance but often fails to create genuine, lasting change in someone's beliefs or behavior. When the manipulated person realizes he has been coerced or deceived, he will likely feel resentful and resistant to further influence.

3. Manipulation does not address the underlying issues or reasons why someone holds a certain belief or behaves in a certain way. Without addressing these root causes, the manipulated change is unlikely to be sustainable or meaningful.

4. Manipulating someone's mind goes against the principles of autonomy and respect for individual choices. People generally value their independence and are more likely to resist manipulation that threatens their sense of individuality.

Alli and Ted's relationship seemed like a fairy tale. However, cracks began to show when Ted's controlling behavior surfaced. He monitored Alli's every move, becoming increasingly possessive and manipulative. At first, Alli brushed off his behavior, hoping it was just a phase. But as time passed, Ted's manipulation intensified. He isolated her from friends and family, making her feel dependent on him for everything. Alli's self-esteem plummeted as she lost her sense of identity. Despite Alli's attempts to confront Ted, he would gaslight her into believing it was all in her head. The toxicity of their relationship continued to escalate until Alli realized she had to break free from his suffocating grip. Finally finding the courage to leave, Alli walked away from the once beautiful love that had turned into a nightmare. It was a painful decision, but she knew she deserved better than a relationship built on control and manipulation. As Alli embarked on a journey of self-discovery and healing, she learned valuable lessons about self-worth and boundaries. And in time, she found a love built on trust, respect, and genuine care.

Manipulation is ineffective in changing someone's mind because it damages trust, fails to create genuine change, neglects underlying issues, and undermines individual freedom. Instead, fostering open communication, building trust, and respecting others' perspectives are more effective ways to influence change.

It is important to understand that there are many variables in life you cannot control—in this case, another person. Finding the root cause could be helpful. This may not always be possible, or even "fix" the strained or ended relationship, but if your situation allows, take some time to discover the root cause.

Ways to discover the root cause:

1. *Communication*: Open and honest communication can help identify underlying issues that caused the relationship to break down. It is key in unraveling the source. By fostering open and honest dialogue, you can express your thoughts, feelings, and concerns, leading to a deeper understanding of each other's perspectives. You can uncover underlying issues that may have contributed to tension or misunderstandings through active listening and empathy. Communication enables the opportunity to address conflicts constructively, find common ground, and work together toward resolution or closure. By sharing openly and authentically, you can build trust, paving the way for healing, growth, and maybe even a stronger bond.

2. *Self-reflection*: Reflect on your behaviors, thoughts, and emotions that may have contributed to the problem. Self-reflection is a powerful tool that can help you delve deep into your thoughts and emotions to identify issues in the breakdown. By taking the time to introspect and analyze your own actions, beliefs, and communication patterns, you can gain valuable insights into how they may have contributed to the deterioration of the relationship. Through self-reflection, you can uncover underlying issues such as unresolved conflicts, unmet needs, or personal insecurities that may have influenced your behaviors and interactions with your partner. By better understanding yourself, you can take responsibility for your actions, make necessary changes, and work toward understanding what went wrong. Self-reflection also promotes empathy and perspective-taking, allowing you to see the situation from your partner's point of view and gain a deeper appreciation for your feelings and needs. By engaging in self-reflection, you can foster personal growth, improve communication, and rebuild trust in relationships.

3. *Seeking feedback*: Asking for feedback from a trusted friend, therapist, counselor, or even ex-partner, if possible, can provide valuable insights into areas needing improvement. If the Missing Variable is open to discussion, delve into the situation with him or her and seek feedback that could bring closure and guide you in future relationships. If you know someone who has shared a similar experience, find time to discuss how he dealt with the painful and uncertain situation, providing empathy for what he experienced while gaining insight and suggestions for your own circumstance.

4. *Identifying patterns*: Recurring patterns or triggers can lead to conflicts and reveal deep-rooted issues. Recognizing patterns in a relationship can serve as a powerful tool for understanding its dynamics and potential breakdown. By identifying these behaviors, reactions, and cycles, you can gain valuable insight into underlying issues that may have contributed to conflict or

disconnection. These patterns may manifest in communication styles, conflict resolution strategies, emotional responses, or even physical interactions. Understanding these patterns can help you pinpoint areas of concern, acknowledge recurring triggers, and work toward more effective solutions for future encounters or relationships. It can also highlight any unhealthy dynamics or communication barriers that may be hindering a relationship's growth and stability. Shining a light on these patterns can foster greater self-awareness, empathy, and collaboration in addressing challenges and strengthening your connection. Doing so, you can take proactive steps toward fostering healthier, more fulfilling connections built on mutual respect, understanding, and growth.

5. *Therapy*: Seeking professional help from a therapist or counselor can provide a safe space to explore the root cause of the relationship issues. Grief is a difficult emotion to navigate. It is essential to allow yourself time to grieve, and along with help in unveiling the concerns, therapy may be a helpful part of this process for grief as well.

6. *Past experiences*: Examining past experiences and how they may affect the current relationship dynamics can illuminate unresolved issues. Reflecting on past experiences can provide valuable insights into the progression of a relationship. By examining the dynamics, interactions, and emotions from earlier stages, you can identify patterns of behavior or communication that may have contributed to the deterioration of the relationship over time. This process of introspection can bring awareness to underlying issues, unmet needs, or unresolved conflicts that have accumulated and eroded the foundation of the relationship. Recognizing these key points can help you understand the root causes of the decline and make informed decisions about how to address them. By analyzing past experiences with a critical and open-minded perspective, you can gain clarity on where things may have gone wrong and

take proactive steps toward rebuilding, repairing, or moving on from the relationship.

7. *Setting boundaries*: Establishing clear boundaries and expectations can help address underlying issues and prevent future conflicts. Clear boundaries help each person understand his or her roles and responsibilities within the relationship, minimizing misunderstandings and the potential for conflict. By clearly defining what behavior is acceptable and what is not, both parties can feel more secure and respected. Setting expectations helps manage each other's needs, goals, and desires. It encourages open communication and allows you to express your needs and concerns effectively. This can lead to better understanding and compromise, reducing the chances of conflicts arising in the future. Clear boundaries and expectations create a sense of stability and predictability within the relationship. This can help build trust and mutual respect, which is essential for repairing a deteriorating relationship. When both parties understand what is expected of them and what is considered acceptable behavior, they are more likely to work toward resolving issues rather than escalating conflicts. Overall, establishing clear boundaries and expectations fosters healthy communication, respect, and understanding in a relationship, which can help address underlying issues and prevent future conflicts from arising.

8. *Apologizing and forgiveness*: Acknowledging mistakes, apologizing, and practicing forgiveness can help heal past wounds and may even move the relationship forward. They play key roles in uncovering underlying issues and preventing future conflicts in a deteriorating relationship by fostering open communication, building trust, and promoting empathy. Apologizing allows you to take responsibility for your actions and acknowledge your impact on the other person. This can lead to a deeper understanding of the root causes of the conflict and help explore the underlying issues that contributed to the breakdown of the relationship. Forgiveness, on the other

hand, enables you to let go of resentment and move forward. It creates a space for healing and rebuilding trust, essential for repairing a damaged relationship or healing unresolved pain. By engaging in these processes, you are more likely to address the core issues that led to the conflict in the first place. This can lead to greater insight into each other's perspectives, increased empathy, and a stronger foundation for resolving conflicts in the future. Apologizing and forgiveness are powerful tools for promoting emotional healing, strengthening relationships, and preventing future conflicts by fostering understanding, empathy, and trust between individuals.

9.   *Gratitude*: If you can take the apology one step further, showing appreciation and gratitude to the person for the good times you had together and for his or her input into the relationship can go a long way toward mending some broken fences and aiding in the healing process. This may even lead to further revelation of hidden issues, exposing them for analysis or evaluation. Practicing gratitude in a broken relationship can help unveil underlying issues by fostering empathy and understanding between partners. By focusing on the positive aspects of the relationship and expressing appreciation for each other, both partners may become more willing to communicate openly and honestly about their feelings and needs. This can lead to a deeper understanding of the root causes of the issues and facilitate productive discussions on how to address them. Gratitude can also help you reflect on your own actions and contributions to the relationship, promoting self-awareness and personal growth. By acknowledging the good in the relationship, you may also gain insight into what you value and need in a partnership, helping you make more informed decisions in future relationships. By cultivating gratitude, you can gain a greater sense of perspective, compassion, and resilience, which can not only aid in healing from the current relationship but also equip you with valuable lessons and tools for fostering healthier connections in the future.

10. *Praying for discernment*: Praying for discernment can be a powerful tool in uncovering the root cause of a broken relationship. By seeking guidance and clarity from God, you can access a deeper level of understanding and insight into the dynamics at play. Through prayer, you can gain a fresh perspective, identify underlying issues, and pinpoint areas that require healing or reconciliation. This spiritual privilege can help you navigate complex emotions, communicate effectively, and make decisions that align with your values and beliefs. Praying for discernment can lead to greater awareness, empathy, and growth, paving the way for healing and restoration in relationships that may be strained or broken.

By delving deep into the root cause of a broken relationship, you can gain a better understanding of yourself and your "ex" partner and even guide you for a future relationship. This can lead to meaningful insights and potential solutions for building healthier interactions. In the aftermath of a shattered bond lies a profound opportunity for self-discovery and reflection. By embarking on a journey to uncover the intricate layers of a broken relationship, you can unearth invaluable insights not only about yourself but also about your former partner or spouse. It is within these introspective moments that growth takes root, nurturing the seeds of wisdom and understanding. As you navigate the labyrinth of emotions and memories, you unveil hidden truths illuminating the path toward healing and personal evolution. With each revelation, you sculpt a clearer image of who you are and who you aspire to be, paving the way for a more profound connection in future relationships. For in the wreckage of the past lies the blueprint for a brighter and more harmonious future, where self-awareness and empathy intertwine to create a foundation built on shared growth and understanding.

Cameron had experienced her fair share of failed relationships in the past, leaving her heartbroken and disillusioned. But instead of letting those setbacks define her, she chose to learn from them and grow. Reflecting on her past mistakes, Cameron realized she had rushed into relationships without truly getting to know the other person. She had ignored red flags and settled for less than she deserved. Determined to change her approach, she decided to take things slowly and prioritize communication and honesty in her new relationships. As she embarked on a new romance, Cameron applied the lessons she had learned. She communicated openly with her partner about her feelings and expectations, setting healthy boundaries from the start. She made an effort to truly understand and support her boyfriend while also staying true to herself. With patience and a newfound sense of self-worth, Cameron found that her new relationship flourished in ways she had never imagined. She felt a deeper connection with her boyfriend and experienced a level of mutual respect and understanding that had been missing in her past relationships. Through her journey of growth and self-discovery, Cameron learned that embracing her past experiences and using them as lessons had paved the way for a more fulfilling and successful relationship.

While self-reflection may bring some understanding to past relationships, it may have no impact on the broken one as well. Value it as a learning experience to take with you for future interactions. The key is to learn from the experience and explore the situations, as experience is the best teacher. You may never know what actually happened and caused the other person to sway. That's okay, too. This may be difficult for your mind to make right with, but it is necessary to let go and move on.

Ways to accept unresolved issues and move on anyway:

1. *Acknowledge your feelings*: Allow yourself to feel the emotions associated with the unresolved issues without judgment.

2. *Practice self-compassion*: Be kind to yourself during this process and understand that it's okay not to have all the answers right away.

3. *Focus on what you can control*: Shift your focus to things within your control rather than dwelling on what you cannot change.

4. *Seek support*: Talk to friends, family, or a therapist to gain perspective and receive emotional support.

5. *Practice mindfulness*: Stay present and in the moment and avoid ruminating on the past or worrying about the future.

6. *Set boundaries*: Establish boundaries with the unresolved issues or people involved to protect your mental and emotional well-being.

7. *Engage in self-care*: Take care of yourself physically, emotionally, and mentally by engaging in activities that bring you joy and relaxation.

8. *Consider professional help*: If the unresolved issues are overwhelming and impacting your daily life, consider seeking professional help from a therapist or counselor.

9. *Practice forgiveness*: Forgive yourself and others involved in the unresolved issues to release any lingering negative emotions and move forward with a sense of peace. This doesn't mean you must agree or even like what they did. Forgiveness will help YOU heal and move on in a healthier way.

10. *Practice gratitude*: Create a daily list of what and for whom you appreciate. Be committed to doing this and open your eyes to everything around you. Add this to your journal. Although it may be difficult to feel grateful after being hurt by someone, embracing gratitude can still offer several benefits to you. Practicing gratitude can help shift your focus from the negative experience toward the positive aspects of your life, promoting emotional well-being and mental health. By acknowledging the good things in your life, you can cultivate a sense of resilience and hope even in challenging times. Expressing gratitude can foster forgiveness and healing. It can help you release negative emotions and resentment toward the person who hurt you, allowing you to move forward with a lighter heart. Gratitude can also strengthen your relationships with others by promoting empathy, compassion, and understanding, which can lead to healthier and more fulfilling connections. Furthermore, practicing gratitude can enhance your ability to find meaning and purpose in difficult situations, enabling you to grow and learn from your experiences. It can also boost your self-esteem and confidence by reminding you of your strengths

and accomplishments, empowering you to navigate through life's adversities with grace and courage.

11. *Strengthen your relationship with God*: A relationship with God can provide comfort, strength, and guidance when dealing with unresolved issues. By seeking solace in faith, you can find a sense of peace and acceptance that helps you cope with difficult emotions. Believing in God's will can offer a perspective that there is a bigger plan at work, allowing you to surrender control over things you cannot change. Through prayer, meditation, and reflection, you can find clarity and inner peace to help you process your unresolved issues. Trusting in God's plan can provide hope and the assurance that there is a purpose behind your struggles, helping you to overcome feelings of helplessness and despair. A relationship with God can also instill values of forgiveness, compassion, and empathy, enabling you to let go of resentment and bitterness toward yourself and others involved in unresolved issues. By embracing these values, you can work toward healing and moving forward with grace and resilience. Ultimately, a relationship with God can serve as a source of strength and comfort, empowering you to accept your unresolved issues, find closure, and embark on a journey of personal growth and transformation.

It takes two giving and committed people to have a successful relationship. This may not always be the case. It may even start that way, but somewhere down the line, something may change. It doesn't mean you haven't contributed faults to the relationship, but once the other person has determined they are finished, they become the Missing Variable. What are things you can do for yourself once the relationship is over?

Healthy ways to move forward after the relationship ends:

1. Allow yourself to grieve and process your emotions. It's important to acknowledge and accept your feelings rather than suppress them. Take time for a good cry or other ways to release the tension and emotions. In your busy life, sometimes it's difficult to find alone time to process these feelings, and they may get bottled up. Be sure to find a way to let them loose rather than fester. Sometimes, well-meaning friends or family may share similar stories about other hurting people in an attempt to remind you that you're not the only one suffering. Yet, it is essential to take some alone time and allow yourself to validate YOUR feelings so you can process them. Your feelings are important, and they are unique to you. Take whatever time you need to validate them while still appreciating the efforts of loving friends and family. As a flight attendant may instruct, secure your own oxygen mask first before helping secure someone else's. You need to be strong enough first in order to share some compassion with others.

2. Focus on self-care activities such as exercising, eating well, getting enough sleep, and practicing relaxation techniques like meditation or deep breathing. Enjoy a detox bath and energize yourself as you drain toxins from your body.

3. In times of heartbreak and uncertainty, turning to prayer and relying on God's strength can provide solace and guidance to navigate the difficult journey of a breakup. Through prayer, you can find peace, comfort, and inner strength to heal your broken heart and find clarity in the midst of confusion. Trusting in God's plan for you can offer hope for a brighter future and a renewed sense of purpose. By seeking God's support through prayer, you can feel His presence in your life, offering love, understanding, and a sense of peace that surpasses all understanding. Letting go of the pain and surrendering your worries to God can help you release the burden you are carrying and find the courage to move forward with grace and resilience.

Through prayer, you can find the strength to forgive, let go of bitterness, and open your heart to new possibilities. By relying on God's guidance, you can emerge from this challenging time with a deeper sense of faith, resilience, and a renewed spirit. Trust in God's love and plan for you, knowing He will lead you through this storm and into a brighter tomorrow.

4. Surround yourself with supportive friends and family members who can provide emotional support during this difficult time.

5. Engage in activities that bring you joy and fulfillment, whether hobbies, volunteering, or exploring new interests.

6. Consider seeking professional help from a therapist or counselor to work through your feelings and gain insight into the breakup.

7. Set boundaries with your ex-partner to give yourself space to heal and move on.

8. Reflect on the lessons learned from the relationship and use them to grow and improve yourself.

9. Avoid rebound relationships and give yourself time to heal before entering a new romantic involvement. Healing after a committed relationship takes a significant amount of time. Love yourself enough to allow this time to self-reflect and heal.

10. Practice self-compassion and be patient with yourself, as healing takes time.

11. Remember that it's okay to seek help and support when needed and that healing is a journey that requires self-care and self-compassion.

Grief:

Grieving is a vital part of the healing process in any loss, especially in human relationships. We are meant to love others and be loved. When a relationship ends because of someone else's decision, even while you may not understand the reasons, it is essential to allow yourself time to grieve for the loss. Everyone grieves in different ways and for various durations of time. Discover how you can effectively grieve and take however much time you need to process your loss.

Why is it important to take time to grieve? Grieving allows for emotional healing and growth. It provides the opportunity to process the range of emotions that come with loss, such as sadness, anger, and confusion. By acknowledging and experiencing these emotions, you can begin to come to terms with the end of the relationship and start to move forward. Grieving also helps in accepting the reality of the situation and letting go of any lingering attachments or hopes for reconciliation. It allows you to reflect on the relationship, learn from the experience, and gain insights into yourself and your needs. By allowing yourself to grieve the loss of a relationship, you can prevent unresolved emotions from impacting future relationships or your overall well-being. It is a natural and necessary part of the healing process that enables you to eventually find closure and open yourself up to new possibilities and connections.

Regret:

What is regret? Regret is a complex and often painful emotion that arises when you feel disappointment or remorse about past actions, decisions, or choices. It involves wishing that things had been different or that you had acted differently in a particular situation. Regret can stem from various sources, such as missed opportunities, mistakes, or the consequences of your actions.

Sometimes, in a Missing Variable situation, you may automatically default to what you "may have" done wrong or could have done better. There is no way of knowing if anything you may have done differently really would have mattered. You must learn not to allow regret to consume you negatively. Regret can be a powerful motivator for personal growth and change, as it can lead you to reflect on your choices and behaviors and make adjustments for the future. However, dwelling on regret excessively can also be detrimental to your mental well-being, leading to feelings of guilt, self-blame, and negativity.

Regret is a common human experience that reminds you of your fallibility and the importance of learning from your past experiences. It is important to acknowledge and process feelings of regret in a healthy way in order to move forward and live more intentionally in the present.

It is important to recognize regret and act on it. To acknowledge and resolve regret from a failed relationship, it is important first to accept and process your emotions. Allow yourself to feel regret, sadness, and any other emotions that arise. Reflect on what you learned from the experience and how it has contributed to your personal growth.

Next, forgive yourself and your ex-partner or spouse for any mistakes made during the relationship. Understand that everyone makes mistakes and is a part of the learning process. Consider seeking support from friends, family, or a therapist to help you work through your emotions and gain perspective. Talking about your feelings with someone you trust can validate them and give you a different outlook on the situation. Focus on self-care and engage in activities that bring you joy and fulfillment. Practice self-compassion and remind yourself that you deserve love and contentment.

Use the experience as an opportunity for growth and self-improvement. Apply the lessons learned to future relationships, setting healthy boundaries, and communicating effectively. Remember that it is okay to feel regret, but it is essential to process these emotions in a healthy way to move forward positively.

Prevention is always better than the cure.

—Jill Fandrich

This quote applies to more than just disease prevention and your physical health. There are ways you can prepare yourself to prevent future feelings of regret.

Ways to prevent regret in relationships:

1. Communicate openly and honestly with your partner to avoid misunderstandings and address issues promptly.

2. Set realistic expectations and boundaries to prevent feelings of disappointment.

3. Value the other person and ensure he or she knows they are treasured, appreciated, and a priority to you. It is Biblical to put the needs of others in front of your own. Use logic and determine when this is appropriate while never allowing yourself to be a "doormat."

4. Prioritize self-care and maintain a healthy balance between personal time and time spent with your partner.

5. Practice empathy and understanding to foster a deeper connection and prevent conflicts.

6. Be willing to compromise and find solutions that work for both you and your partner.

7. Take responsibility for your actions and apologize when necessary to prevent resentment from building up.

8. Reflect on past relationships and learn from them to make better choices in the future.

9. Seek support from friends, family, or a therapist to gain different perspectives and maintain emotional well-being.

10. Avoid making impulsive decisions based on emotions. Emotions are subjective and often circumstantial. Take time to think things through. Use critical thinking to make logical and well-thought-out decisions.

11. Remember that it's okay to walk away from toxic or unhealthy relationships to prioritize your own well-being and sanity.

It's important to recognize that sometimes things are just out of your control. In this chapter, we discussed relationships and how the Missing Variable is the other person's thoughts, opinions, and actions differing from yours. We looked at how to move forward, heal from the situation, acknowledge grief, and even ways to avoid future regret. Relationships that end "without our permission" are hurtful and lead to a gamut of emotions that are important to process immediately for your health and well-being and that of your future relationships.

For in the wreckage of the past lies the blueprint for a brighter and more harmonious future, where self-awareness and empathy intertwine to create a foundation built on shared growth and understanding.

—Jill Fandrich

In the tapestry of life, grief, guilt, and regret are threads that weave a complex pattern of experience. Embrace them with compassion, for they are the colors that give depth to your inner landscape. Acknowledge their presence and learn from them, but do not let them consume you. Instead, use them as stepping stones toward healing and growth. Remember, the beauty of a tapestry lies not in its individual threads but in the harmony of its interwoven stories. Your journey through grief, guilt, and regret is a chapter in your story, not the end of it. Allow yourself to feel, forgive, and let go, for only then can you find peace and move forward with grace and wisdom.

—Jill Fandrich

Reflect:

1. Recall a relationship where you felt you acted appropriately, gave sacrificially, and appreciated wholeheartedly, yet the person ultimately chose to walk away. How did this make you feel? How did you respond? What was the result of your response? Journal your answers.

2. How do you allow yourself to grieve? How do you handle guilt and regret? What changes will you make as a result of this chapter? What would you have done differently? Journal your answers.

3. What challenges are involved with any of the changes? How will you overcome them? What resources will you add to make this most effective? Journal your answers.

4. What are some dangers of not making any changes in how you respond in relationships? What are some of the benefits of making changes? Journal regarding the behaviors and techniques you will implement for future relationships.

5. Observe your interactions with other people throughout each day. What seems to be effective? What doesn't seem to be working? Compare the differences and journal your thoughts on them. What do you notice?

6. Find ways to program effective grief, guilt, and regret resolutions into your "preprogram." More information about how to "Reprogram Your Pre-Program" is found in *Elevate Your Mind to Success, Success Is Ele-MENTAL*, and at www. DrJillFandrich.com.

7. How will you utilize these skills in other areas of your life? Journal your answers.

8. Who will you share this information with? Who will benefit most from it? Journal your answers.

9. Apply critical thinking to the information you learned. More about critical thinking is found in *Who Connects Your Dots?, Medically Speaking, Who Connects Your Dots?*, and *Students: Who Connects Your Dots?*

10. Practice the skills you learned daily. Journal and monitor your progress.

CHAPTER 3

CASE STUDY TWO: THE (UN)PERFECT PLANS

Have you ever made the most organized and fool-proof plan only to find everything fell through at the last minute? I frowned at the early sound of my alarm—3 a.m., to be exact. I slowly stretched, then darted out of bed and prepped for the trip ahead. I stuffed the last of my necessities into my third piece of luggage, and off to the airport I went. A neighbor was kind enough to drop me off at the departure port of the airport, and the outdoor concierge was eager to toss two pieces of my luggage on the conveyor belt for a generous tip in hand.

Once through security, I steered my way to the terminal and found I had a few minutes to spare. After one last restroom break, I joined the line for a tasty grande mocha delight, then worked my way back to the departure gate to wait out the final twenty minutes until boarding began. Everything was going *just as planned!*

The 737 left right on schedule from RSW in Fort Myers and landed at the Atlanta ATL airport with forty minutes to spare before the next 747 was to taxi and fly me off to the awaiting adventures in LA for the upcoming week. To my delight, the departing gate had just been changed from a subway ride away to the gate right next door to the arriving terminal! How perfectly everything was going!

I settled within the newly selected neighboring gate, all set to board for the next part of the journey, and anticipated a lazy and restful four-hour trip. I was to arrive three hours "in the past" since we were flying three time zones away. It would be 10 a.m. in LA, and since I couldn't check in to the hotel until 3 p.m., I had scheduled a drive to Newport Beach and lunch with friends at an iconic restaurant there. A perfect plan had been prepared! I boarded the plane and settled in with the door sealed, the seatbelt fastened, and the tray table "in its upright position," just as instructed. Then—it happened. The plan went awry. What were we waiting for? What was taking so long? Finally, a hesitant voice bellowed through the speakers, indicating a mechanical problem would cause us all to be "*unboarding*" the plane, and there was no new plane yet in sight. Delayed!

This one incident set off a chain reaction involving plans made with other people, the shuttle to the car rental offsite location, the car rental reservation itself, and the plans for the day in general. All were affected negatively despite the best-laid plans. What could I have done differently? Nothing. And what was the Missing Variable? The unexpected mechanical problem and the lack of a backup plane.

Sometimes, things beyond your control occur no matter how much time and effort you put into planning, scheduling, reservations, and appointments. Think of a time when you created a "master plan," and the plan did not fall into place as expected despite your careful consideration. What was the scenario? What did you expect to happen? What actually happened? What could you have done differently? Was it a case similar to the story just mentioned, where you did everything correctly, yet something went wrong along the way?

How flexible are you when things don't go the way you have planned? Are you able to adapt and create a new plan? Emotionally, how do you respond when things are altered from expectations? How can you be more prepared to expect the unexpected?

Flexibility is a character quality that involves the ability to adapt, adjust, and be open to change in various situations. When you possess flexibility, you are able to embrace uncertainty, remain open-minded, and navigate challenges with ease. You are willing to consider different perspectives, compromise when necessary, and find creative solutions to problems. Flexibility also involves being able to go with the flow, make quick decisions, and handle unexpected changes with grace.

Flexibility makes you more resilient, adaptable, and able to thrive in dynamic environments. It allows you to balance structure with spontaneity and adjust plans and goals as needed. Flexibility is a valuable trait in personal and professional relationships, as it fosters collaboration, teamwork, and effective communication. It is a strength that allows you to stay agile, positive, and proactive in the face of challenges and opportunities.

Liz was a meticulous planner, mapping out every detail of her life to avoid any surprises. However, one day, her carefully crafted plans were thrown into disarray when her car broke down on the way to an important job interview. Instead of panicking, Liz took a deep breath and assessed her options. She decided to walk to the nearest bus stop and catch a ride to the interview. Arriving late and flustered, Liz was worried that the opportunity was lost. To her surprise, the interviewer was impressed by her calm demeanor and ability to adapt to unexpected circumstances. He explained that the company valued flexibility and problem-solving skills and offered Liz the job on the spot. Liz realized that sometimes, being flexible and open to change can lead to even better outcomes than sticking rigidly to a plan. Embracing the unexpected had not only saved her in a difficult situation but had also opened up a new and exciting opportunity she hadn't anticipated. From that day on, Liz learned to loosen her grip on her plans and be open to the possibilities that come with being flexible and adaptable in any situation.

How can you become more flexible when faced with an unexpected challenge?

1. *Expect the unexpected:* When you have a mindset that things may not always go as expected, your subconscious is already in action, creating alternate plans that could help your day run smoothly if faced with an unplanned event.

2. *Maintain a positive mindset:* View obstacles as opportunities for growth and learning rather than setbacks. If possible, find enjoyment in the challenge. This builds resilience and resourcefulness, both of which are strong character qualities.

3. *Stay calm and composed:* Take a deep breath and assess the situation rationally before taking any action. Have a plan for ways to calm yourself. This certainly wasn't the first time the unexpected happened. Learn what works best for you and resort to calming ways instantly when faced with obstacles.

4. *Embrace adaptability:* Be willing to adjust your plans and strategies to overcome the obstacle effectively. This may not actually be a

choice! So, the more readily you accept the idea of adjusting, the better prepared you will be for a favorable outcome.

5. *Seek alternative solutions*: Be open to exploring different approaches or perspectives to find a solution. Let's face it: there is a great chance of a delayed flight in the first case study presented. Delays seem to occur more and more frequently, so when flying, be flexible and have backup plans in place. Liz didn't hesitate to problem-solve in her situation. Her ability to adapt quickly led to a new job opportunity.

6. *Utilize your support system*: Reach out to friends, colleagues, or mentors for advice and guidance. Have phone numbers available to help where needed. Have a list of all contacts for the present day and even the following day handy to reach out to and adjust plans. Or have another support system ready to help with plans if need be.

7. *Practice mindfulness*: Stay present in the moment and focus on what you can control instead of worrying about what you cannot. This is a good time to practice patience and awareness.

8. *Reflect on past experiences*: Draw from previous challenges you have overcome to boost your confidence in handling new obstacles. Reflecting before your trip can also help you have a sound backup plan in place.

9. *Learn from the experience*: Use setbacks as opportunities to learn and grow, improving your resilience for future challenges. Be intentional in your desire to develop more creativity and resourcefulness. By incorporating these strategies into your approach, you can enhance your flexibility and better navigate unexpected obstacles confidently and effectively. Everything happens for a reason. Perhaps there is someone you are meant to meet or even avoidance of something due to delaying your journey. Accept the circumstances and look for opportunities to expand your network of people and experiences.

When the news of the delay was announced, I instinctively observed the reactions of the other passengers. Naturally, frustration was a typical response. But what is always interesting to me is that, for the most part, the majority of passengers seem to adjust fairly well to extenuating circumstances. There is likely a small group with an inflexible deadline and can't afford to miss connections or appointments, which is certainly understandable. I am amazed that most passengers find a way to resolve the situation respectably.

What are other ways you choose to calm yourself? Is it different for various situations? How effective is it? Are you triggered instantly to begin these methods when obstacles arise? What is your most effective way? Have you ever practiced mindfulness? What is mindfulness?

Mindfulness is the practice of being fully present and aware of your thoughts, feelings, sensations, and surroundings without judgment. In unexpected situations, mindfulness can help you relax by allowing you to stay calm, focused, and grounded in the present moment. Practicing mindfulness can create a sense of inner peace and stability even when faced with challenging or uncertain circumstances.

Techniques such as deep breathing, body scan meditation, and observing your thoughts without attachment can help you stay centered and prevent overwhelming stress or anxiety. Mindfulness can also help you cultivate resilience and adaptability, enabling you to respond to unexpected situations with clearer thinking and emotional balance. By acknowledging your feelings and thoughts without getting swept away by them, you can navigate unexpected events with greater ease and composure. Incorporating mindfulness into your daily routine through meditation, breathing exercises, or simply taking moments to pause and tune into your senses can effectively support you in relaxing and finding calmness in the face of unexpected situations.

Stan, a busy executive, found himself in a high-pressure meeting that was not going as planned. Feeling overwhelmed and on the verge of losing his composure, he remembered the mindfulness techniques he had been practicing. Taking a deep breath, Stan closed his eyes and focused on the sensation of his breath entering and leaving his body. He let go of the racing thoughts and brought his attention to the present moment. As he grounded himself in the here and now, his body began to relax, and his mind grew clearer. With a calmer demeanor, Stan was able to respond to the challenges in the meeting with a greater sense of clarity and perspective. He listened attentively, choosing his words thoughtfully instead of reacting impulsively. By staying present and mindful, Stan navigated the meeting with grace and composure. Despite the stressful situation, he maintained his inner peace and found solutions to the problems at hand. As Stan left the meeting, he felt a sense of accomplishment and gratitude for the mindfulness practice that had helped him stay calm and focused when it mattered most.

Have you ever had a delayed situation happen to you? What was your Missing Variable? What other scenarios involved altered plans? What were the Missing Variables involved in each case? Did you recognize them as situations that were beyond your control? The response to any situation outside of your control may be similar. For example, it is always important to stay flexible and adaptive. Remain calm, take a moment to process the change, and avoid reacting impulsively. Assess the situation to understand the reasons behind the change and how it impacts your original plans.

When situations are unexpectedly altered, reach out to those involved to discuss the new circumstances and determine the next steps. Modify your plans as needed to accommodate the change, considering any constraints or new requirements. Maintain a positive attitude and focus on finding solutions rather than dwelling on setbacks. Learn from the experience. Reflect on how you handled the change and identify any lessons or improvements for future situations. Remember that unexpected changes are a part of life, and your ability to be flexible, adapt, and respond thoughtfully can lead to successful outcomes despite the disruption.

Reflect:

1. Recall a situation where you put a significant amount of time, effort, and even research into creating a perfect plan, yet things did not go accordingly. How did this make you feel? How did you respond? What was the result of your response? Journal your answers.

2. What changes will you make to future plans as a result of this chapter? What would you have done differently? Journal your answers.

3. What challenges are involved with any of the changes? How will you overcome them? What resources will you add to make this most effective? Journal your answers.

4. What are some of the dangers of not being flexible? What are some of the benefits of it? Recall a situation when you were not flexible in your responses. What would you change? Now, recall a situation where you chose to adapt. What did you do well? Journal regarding the behaviors and techniques you will implement for future important planned events.

5. Observe your responses to unexpected changes throughout each day. What seems to be an effective response? What doesn't seem to be effective? Compare the differences and journal your thoughts on the key differences. What do you notice?

6. Find ways to program mindfulness, patience, flexibility, and awareness into your "preprogram." More information about how to "Reprogram Your Pre-Program" is found in *Elevate Your Mind to Success, Success Is Ele-MENTAL*, and at www. DrJillFandrich.com.

7. How will you utilize these skills in other areas of your life? Journal your answers.

8. Who will you share this information with? Who will benefit most from it? Journal your answers.

9. Apply critical thinking to the information you learned. More about critical thinking is found in *Who Connects Your Dots?*, *Medically Speaking, Who Connects Your Dots?*, and *Students: Who Connects Your Dots?*

10. Practice the skills you learned daily. Journal and monitor your progress.

CHAPTER 4

CASE STUDY THREE: "BUSH-LEAGUE" BOSSES

Kim had continuously poured her heart and soul into her work at the company. She arrived early, stayed late, and constantly went above and beyond to deliver exceptional results. However, despite her dedication and hard work, she found herself constantly overlooked and unappreciated by her colleagues and superiors. Despite the lack of recognition, Kim remained determined to prove her worth. She continued to strive for excellence in every task she took on, hoping eventually, her efforts would be acknowledged. As the months turned into years, Kim's frustration grew. She watched as others received praise and promotions while she remained stagnant in her position. She felt disheartened and demotivated, but deep down, she knew she couldn't give up. But now what?

Have you ever worked for a company and poured your heart, soul, and time into it only to realize you and your work were unnoticed, unappreciated, or worse yet, your work was "claimed" by someone else? I worked for a company that ran many different clinics and was put in charge of four of them. As it turned out, my "boss" lacked leadership skills and abandoned me at my clinics, and I was thrown into a situation of search and discovery on my own. As I am quite resourceful and intelligent, I did just that. I wasn't afraid to ask questions of those around me and gather information. I researched through relevant sources inside and outside the company to find the best information and found out what it took to run the clinics successfully.

The clinics grew and thrived. I soon realized the fourth clinic was actually "in need" of my credentials and status, as my boss had a criminal record, and permitting the clinic required a forensic background check. I was asked to represent the company for this check, and naturally, I agreed.

I continued to work hard for this company and displayed integrity, loyalty, diligence, and resourcefulness, always meeting deadlines and giving selflessly. My "boss" remained nonexistent at any of the four clinics. In a four-year time frame, she never even once evaluated my performance, as per company policy, which was to be quarterly. She never took any time to review what I was doing, show appreciation for my having figured out most things independently, and acknowledge that I grew the clinics successfully in both numbers and morale. They were well-run, and the patients and staff were thriving.

I approached my boss openly, courteously, and respectfully, sharing how her actions and responses negatively affected me. She suddenly began to micromanage and mistreat me, making false accusations, changing well-run procedures, and chasing many loyal, hardworking employees away.

In another scenario, an employee named Sarah worked tirelessly at a small marketing firm. She consistently went above and beyond her duties, coming up with innovative ideas and working late to meet deadlines. Despite her dedicated efforts, her boss, Mr. Thompson, was incompetent and often took credit for her work. Sarah felt frustrated and unappreciated, but she didn't let it deter her from giving her best. One day, a major project was assigned to her, and she poured all her creativity and hard work into it. When the project was a huge success, Mr. Thompson once again claimed the glory as his own.

Feeling disheartened, Sarah decided it was time to confront her boss. She calmly explained how his lack of recognition affected her morale and motivation. Surprisingly, Mr. Thompson listened attentively and realized his mistake. From that day on, he acknowledged Sarah's contributions publicly and started recognizing her hard work. Sarah's dedication and perseverance had finally paid off, and she felt valued and appreciated in the workplace once again. They soon developed a better working relationship built on mutual respect and appreciation.

In the previous scenarios, Sarah and I worked diligently and with integrity for incompetent and unappreciative bosses. The work ethic and environments were comparable. Generally, you would think that if you work hard, boost team morale, and produce favorable results, you would be recognized and even celebrated by an effective and influential leader. However, in each of these scenarios, that was not the case. What or who would you say is the Missing Variable in each of these stories? Incompetent bosses.

In a professional setting, it can be frustrating when, despite consistently performing at a high level and executing tasks flawlessly, your efforts go unrecognized by an incompetent boss. This could be due to various reasons, such as their lack of understanding or visibility into your contributions, personal biases, or their own insecurities. To navigate this situation, focusing on what you can control is important. Clearly communicate your accomplishments and the value you bring to the team in a respectful and assertive manner. Document your achievements and contributions, giving you tangible evidence to showcase when needed. Seek feedback from colleagues or mentors who can validate and support your work.

It may also be beneficial to be bold and have an open and honest conversation with your boss about your concerns, highlighting the impact of recognition on your motivation and morale. However, if, despite your best efforts, recognition continues to elude you, it might be time to reassess your career goals and consider alternative paths where your efforts are appreciated and rewarded. Remember, your worth is not defined by the recognition you receive at work, and it's essential to prioritize your own growth and well-being.

Boldness is a character quality with several benefits. When used in the correct context, it can lead to increased confidence and self-assurance, enabling you to take risks and face challenges with courage, such as approaching your boss. This can result in personal growth and development as you push yourself out of your comfort zone. Boldness can also foster innovation and creativity as you are more willing to explore new ideas and think outside the box. It can lead to seizing opportunities that others may shy away from, driving success and achievement. Being bold can help in standing out from the crowd and making a lasting impression in various aspects of life, such as career advancement, relationships, and personal goals. It can also inspire others and create a positive impact by setting an example of fearlessness and determination.

Notice how two different and seemingly incompetent bosses can respond in strikingly different ways. Initially, they responded in a similar manner. Then, when approached appropriately with a valid concern, one responded defensively and irrationally, and the other recognized his incompetence and inappropriate behavior and then responded as an effective leader.

The nature of a boss is beyond your control. It is a Missing Variable. But often, it is helpful to understand why someone may respond the way they do. This provides insight and information to help you make decisions about your own well-being and future when working for such a boss.

Reasons bosses may act defensively rather than display leadership qualities:

1. *Insecurity:* Bosses may feel threatened by criticism or challenges to their authority, leading them to react defensively to protect their egos. Incompetent bosses may feel insecure for several reasons. First, they may be aware of their own shortcomings and fear being exposed or criticized by their team. They may worry about job security and feel threatened by more competent employees. Incompetent bosses may also lack self-confidence and feel unsure of their abilities, leading to feelings of inadequacy and insecurity. Additionally, they may feel pressure to perform well and meet expectations, which can be overwhelming when they lack the necessary skills or knowledge. Incompetent bosses may also compare themselves to their more competent colleagues and feel inferior, leading to feelings of insecurity and self-doubt. They may struggle with "imposter syndrome," feeling like they don't deserve their position or are not qualified for their role. This can create a cycle of self-doubt and insecurity, contributing to their lack of confidence. Overall, insecurity in incompetent bosses may stem from a combination of self-awareness of their shortcomings, fear of failure, lack of self-confidence, pressure to perform, and comparison to others.

2. *Fear of failure:* Bosses may be afraid of making mistakes or being seen as inadequate, causing them to avoid taking risks or seeking feedback. This goes back to feelings of insecurity.

3. *Lack of self-awareness*: Some bosses may have a limited understanding of their own behavior and its impact on others, which can result in defensive reactions to situations.

4. *Poor communication skills*: Difficulty in effectively communicating thoughts and emotions can lead to misunderstandings and defensive responses.

5. *Stress and pressure*: High levels of stress or pressure can cause bosses to become more reactive and defensive in their interactions with others.

6. *Past experiences*: Previous negative experiences or traumas could influence a boss's behavior, making them more likely to respond defensively in certain situations.

7. *Organizational culture*: The overall culture of the workplace may promote defensiveness over open communication and collaboration, influencing the boss's behavior accordingly.

Despite feeling unappreciated by your boss, focus on things you can control. Remaining diligent and professional in your work is important. Focus on your own personal standards of excellence and take pride in your work for your own satisfaction. Seek feedback from coworkers or mentors who can provide constructive criticism and support. Remember that your work ethic and dedication reflect your own integrity and professionalism, regardless of external recognition.

Continue to communicate openly with your boss about your accomplishments and contributions, highlighting your value to the team. Try to understand your boss's perspective and motivations, and look for ways to improve your relationship with him or her. If necessary, consider discussing your concerns with HR to address any issues affecting your work environment. Maintain a positive attitude and seek opportunities for growth and development within the company. Take on new challenges and responsibilities to showcase your skills and commitment. Remember that your worth is not defined solely by your boss's recognition but by your own perseverance and dedication to your work.

You are not responsible for your boss's behavior or responses, as each person is accountable for his own actions and decisions. Your boss has unique experiences, values, and perspectives that shape how he behaves and interacts with others. It is important to recognize that you cannot control or predict how your boss will respond to certain situations, as his actions are influenced by various factors beyond your control.

It is crucial to focus on what you can control, such as your own actions, communication style, and work performance, rather than trying to anticipate or manage your boss's behavior. By maintaining professionalism, open communication, and a positive attitude, you can navigate the relationship with your boss effectively, even if you cannot predict the specific responses. Remember that everyone is entitled to their own opinions and behaviors, and it is not your responsibility to change or manage them. Focus on excelling in your role, fostering a positive work environment, and constructively addressing any concerns or conflicts.

The actions of others do not define your worth. It is your decision where you choose to work, and you deserve to be valued wherever you go. Your work is valuable, and your unique skills and talents should be recognized and appreciated. Don't settle for anything less. You have the power to choose where you invest your time and energy. Surround yourself with those who appreciate your contributions and watch your potential soar. In a world full of opportunities, never forget that you hold the key to your own success. Choose to work where your value is acknowledged and celebrated. Your worth is non-negotiable. Stand tall, be proud of your work, and choose an environment that uplifts and respects your worth. Remember, you are in control of your own destiny, and your value is immeasurable. Choose wisely where you invest your time and talents.

 Reflect:

1. Recall a situation where you put significant time and effort into a work project, yet you were unappreciated by your boss. How about a time when you were unnoticed? Have you ever had your work claimed or accredited to someone else? How did this make you feel? How did you respond? What was the result of your response? Journal your answers.

2.   What have you learned about your work environment? How does your boss compare to the ones mentioned in this chapter? What changes will you make as a result of this chapter? Journal your answers.

3.   What challenges are involved with any of the changes? How will you overcome them? What resources will you add to make this most effective? Journal your answers.

4.   What are some potential consequences of not making any changes? What are some of the benefits of making changes? Journal your answers.

5.   Observe your responses to lack of recognition or appreciation throughout each day. What seems to be an effective response? What makes it effective? What doesn't seem to be effective? Compare the differences and journal your thoughts on the key differences. What do you notice?

6.   Find ways to program boldness, assertiveness, and courage into your "preprogram." More information about how to "Reprogram Your Pre-Program" is found in *Elevate Your Mind to Success, Success Is Ele-MENTAL*, and at www.DrJillFandrich.com.

7.   How will you utilize these skills in other areas of your life? Journal your answers.

8.   Who will you share this information with? Who will benefit most from it? Journal your answers.

9.   Apply critical thinking to the information you learned. More about critical thinking is found in *Who Connects Your Dots?, Medically Speaking, Who Connects Your Dots?*, and *Students: Who Connects Your Dots?*

10. Practice the skills you learned daily. Journal and monitor your progress.

CHAPTER 5

CASE STUDY FOUR: SUDDEN DEATH

In a small town, a young and well-known man named Ethan was known for his vibrant energy and zest for life. He was always the first to tackle a new adventure and lived each day to the fullest. His friends and family were in awe of his vitality and spirit. One day, tragedy struck when Ethan collapsed suddenly while out for a run. Despite being young and in excellent health, he was pronounced dead at the scene. The doctors were baffled, unable to find any explanation for his sudden passing. His family was left devastated and bewildered by the unexpected loss of such a vibrant soul.

Do you know anyone who was young, in the prime of life, exercised, seemed to have an overall healthy lifestyle, etc., yet died suddenly for no "apparent" reason? This person appeared to be doing everything right. However, without any warning or logical reasoning, they died "inexplicably."

When someone you know dies unexpectedly, you may feel shocked, confused, grieved, and overwhelmed by a flood of emotions. You may experience disbelief, denial, and a profound sense of loss. The sudden nature of the death can leave you feeling stunned and struggling to make sense of what has happened. There may be feelings of guilt, regret, and unfinished business, as well as a deep sense of sadness and grief.

You may even feel a range of emotions, such as anger, frustration, or helplessness at the sudden loss of a loved one. The unexpected death can also disrupt feelings of security and stability, leading to anxiety and fear about the future. You may struggle to come to terms with the reality of the situation and may find it challenging to process your emotions. It is hard to accept and comprehend a loss you weren't prepared for.

In the previous story, or one you have that is similar, what is the Missing Variable? God's will? What you do know is the person's passing is out of your control. God's will is the divine plan or intention for humanity and the universe. It is the guiding force that shapes the destiny of people and the world. It is, therefore, essential to discern and follow God's will, emphasizing prayer, meditation, and ethical principles to align yourself with it. The concept of God's will is a source of comfort and guidance for believers, providing a sense of purpose and direction in life. However, interpreting and understanding God's will can be complex and subjective, as it involves grappling with questions of free will, destiny, and the nature of God's relationship with creation. Ultimately, God's will can be found by reading, studying, and immersing yourself in the Bible, God's Word. Being deeply rooted in faith and spirituality can serve as a source of inspiration and motivation for people seeking to live according to their beliefs and values.

While a sudden death is beyond your control, processing your emotions is within your control. However, these are often complicated emotions that need to be resolved. For example, sometimes there is lingering guilt if you had a recent quarrel with this person or didn't spend the quality time with them that you would have liked to. Or perhaps you neglected to tell them how you felt, not realizing the unusually shortened timeframe. How can you begin to process these feelings? Start by understanding that these feelings are normal and a part of the grieving process.

Ways to work through guilt or remorse following the death of a loved one:

1. *Acknowledge your feelings*: Allow yourself to feel guilty or remorseful without judgment. Recognize that these emotions are a natural response to loss.

2. *Seek support*: Talk to a trusted friend, family member, therapist, or support group. Sharing your feelings can help you process them and gain perspective. It is important not to be alone during this vulnerable and emotional time. Venting is therapeutic and a part of the healing process.

3. Reflect on your actions: Consider whether you feel guilty about specific things and whether they are within your control. Focus on what you can learn from the situation rather than blaming yourself.

4. *Practice self-compassion*: Be kind to yourself and practice self-care. Remember that it's okay to grieve and that you are not alone. Take as much time as you need to heal. Everyone processes a loss differently, and you need to do the same.

5. *Honoring their memory*: Find healthy ways to honor your loved one's memory, such as creating a tribute, participating in activities they enjoyed, or volunteering in their name. This isn't for them but rather to help you heal. It's important to validate your love for them however you feel best doing it. You can even honor them by spending quality time with other people you haven't spent time with in a while. Use this unfortunate event to make improvements in other relationships in honor of the lost loved one.

6. *Forgive yourself*: As the saying goes, "*Hindsight is 20/20.*" If you knew then what you know now, you would likely do some things differently. This is also out of your control. You cannot change the past. Understand that you made the best choices at the time with the information you had. Forgive yourself of any guilt. As mentioned, you could always "pay forward" this guilt and honor the memory of the lost one or work to improve other relationships, also in their memory.

7. *Seek professional help*: If feelings of guilt or remorse become overwhelming or interfere with your daily life, consider seeking help from a therapist or counselor. Remember, healing takes time, and seeking help as you navigate your emotions is okay. Processing a loss is an arduous and lengthy journey.

Along with feelings of guilt and remorse, there may be frustration or helplessness. Have these feelings been a part of your complex combination of emotions with the loss of a loved one? How did you untangle some of these feelings? What did you do to process them? Did you find it effective? There is no right or wrong process for this; rather, discover what works best for you. Begin again by understanding these feelings are a natural part of the grieving process. Allow yourself to feel these emotions and not suppress them.

Ways to process feelings of frustration or helplessness after the sudden loss of a loved one:

1. *Acknowledge and accept your emotions*: Feeling frustrated and helpless during this difficult time is okay. Cry, vent, or somehow let your emotions run free. This is therapeutic to the healing process and must be acknowledged and addressed.

2. *Express your feelings*: Talk to a trusted friend, family member, or therapist about your emotions. Writing in a journal or engaging in activities like art or music can also help you express your feelings.

3. *Practice self-care*: Take care of yourself by getting enough rest, eating well, and engaging in activities that bring you comfort and relaxation.

4. *Seek support*: Surround yourself with a support system of people who can offer understanding and compassion.

5. *Consider professional help*: If you find it difficult to cope with your emotions, consider seeking the help of a therapist or counselor who specializes in grief and loss. There are community programs that offer grief support you may find locally. You will find people there who share similar experiences as you are going through. You never have to be alone. Remember that healing from loss takes time, and it is important to be patient and kind to yourself as you navigate through this challenging period.

6. *Help others*: Although it may be difficult even to conceive as you are grieving, help someone else. It can be therapeutic and even rewarding to help another person in need. By focusing on someone else's needs, your sad emotions could be uplifted. This isn't meant to replace your grieving process but to

supplement it and give you hope and encouragement through the eyes of another.

7. *Put your anxiety in God's hands*: Place your faith in God and leave all of your frustration, fear, and anxiety on His altar. Pray for peace, healing, and contentment, and trust in His promise to comfort you.

Ways to handle feelings of insecurity and instability about the future after the death of a loved one:

1. *Acknowledge your emotions*: Just as with sifting through other emotions, allow yourself to grieve and process your feelings of insecurity and instability. It's important to recognize and validate your emotions. Challenge these feelings and attempt to find the source. Question each one for the truthfulness of it and whether or not it is really true. Work to find an answer for each one and create a resolution plan if necessary. Journal your responses, concerns, questions, and progress.

2. *Seek support*: Surround yourself with friends and family who can provide emotional support and stability. Consider talking to a therapist or counselor who can help you work through your feelings. Having someone you can vent to and share your deepest concerns is essential.

3. *Take care of yourself*: Engage in self-care activities such as exercising, meditation, journaling, praying, or spending time in nature. Taking care of your physical and emotional well-being is crucial during this time. Discover what you enjoy and even what helps you put things in an appropriate perspective. Be kind and patient with yourself.

4. *Focus on the present*: Try to stay grounded in the present moment and practice mindfulness. This involves being fully engaged in the current moment without judgment. Mindfulness can be achieved through activities like deep breathing, meditation, or simply paying attention to your surroundings. Another helpful technique is to set specific goals or priorities

for the day and stay organized to prevent distractions. Limiting multitasking and practicing active listening can also help you stay present in conversations and tasks. Regular breaks to rest and recharge can improve your focus and prevent overwhelming feelings. It's important to let go of thoughts about the past or get too caught up in worrying about the future, as it can exacerbate feelings of insecurity. Instead, embrace the present moment with gratitude and awareness. Incorporating these strategies into your daily routine can cultivate a greater sense of calm and clarity, leading to improved focus and overall well-being.

5.   *Set small goals*: It's okay to seek help and take things one step at a time as you navigate this difficult period. Break down your long-term goals into smaller, achievable steps. Setting small goals after losing a loved one can provide a sense of stability and structure and build confidence during a difficult time. You can regain a sense of control and accomplishment by breaking down larger tasks into smaller, manageable steps. These small goals can be as simple as getting out of bed at a certain time each day, taking a short walk, or completing a household chore. Focusing on achievable objectives can gradually rebuild your confidence and motivation. Setting small goals can help you create a routine and establish a sense of purpose, which can be crucial for coping with grief. Overall, small goal-setting can provide a sense of direction and progress, contributing to a feeling of stability and hope during the grieving process.

Understanding the loss of a loved one is crucial for emotional healing and growth. It is a natural part of the human experience and contributes to your overall emotional well-being. By acknowledging and processing these feelings, you can come to terms with your grief and begin to heal. While the loss itself may be out of your control, how you choose to cope and move forward is within your power. Developing an understanding of your emotions can help you navigate the grieving process in a healthy way. It allows you to honor the memory of your loved one while also finding ways to cope with the pain and adjust to life without them.

Understanding the loss of a loved one can deepen your appreciation for life and your relationships with others. It can teach you valuable lessons about the impermanence of life and the importance of cherishing the moments you have with those you care about. Understanding the loss of a loved one is an essential part of the healing process, enabling you to find peace, acceptance, and even growth in the face of profound grief.

Recognizing that God's ways differ from yours involves acknowledging that His plans and intentions may not always align with your understanding or expectations. This understanding requires humility, faith, and trust in God's wisdom and sovereignty. It involves accepting that God's ways are higher and more complex than your own limited perspectives and that He works in mysterious ways that may not always make sense to you in the present moment. By recognizing this, you can cultivate a deeper reliance on God, surrendering control and seeking His guidance in all aspects of life. Embracing the idea that His ways are beyond your comprehension can lead to a greater sense of peace, contentment, and spiritual growth as you learn to walk in faith and obedience to Him.

A Bible verse that speaks about God's ways being different than yours is Isaiah 55:8-9 (ESV), which says, "*For my thoughts are not your thoughts, neither are your ways my ways, declares the LORD. For as the heavens are higher than the earth, so are my ways higher than your ways and my thoughts than your thoughts.*" This verse emphasizes the incomprehensible nature of God's wisdom and the vast difference between His perspectives and yours. It encourages you to trust in God's perfect plans and to acknowledge that His ways are beyond your understanding.

Routines are also things to consider when coping with a loss. Losing a loved one can disrupt the comfortable habits and routines that once brought a sense of stability and comfort. The absence of their presence can leave a void in daily life, from simple routines like sharing meals to more significant traditions like weekend outings or family gatherings. Adjusting to life without these familiar habits can be disorienting and overwhelming, highlighting the profound impact of grief. The empty spaces left by their absence may serve as constant reminders of the void they have left behind. Coping with this aspect of grief involves finding new ways to navigate daily life, establishing new routines, and learning to cherish memories while adjusting to a new normal. While the pain of loss may never fully dissipate, finding solace in the memories of shared habits and creating new rituals can help in the healing process.

Grieving the loss of a pet and a loved one share similarities in the emotional process despite the different relationships. Both experiences can evoke feelings of sadness, denial, guilt, anger, and acceptance. The bond formed with a pet or loved one can result in deep emotional attachment, making the loss difficult to cope with.

The grieving process for both often involves going through stages of mourning, adjusting to life without the presence of the pet or loved one, and finding ways to incorporate the memories into daily life. Healing from the loss involves acknowledging the pain, seeking support from others, and allowing yourself to feel and express emotions. Memories of the pet or loved one may bring both joy and sadness, but over time, healing can occur through acceptance and finding ways to honor and remember the relationship. While the loss of a pet and a loved one are distinct experiences, the grieving and healing processes can be similar in the emotional journey toward acceptance and finding peace. Ensure you allow yourself the time to grieve each one, focusing on what is within your control.

Reflect:

1.   Recall a situation where you lost a loved one or pet. Describe the different emotions you felt. How did you respond? What was the Missing Variable? Did you accept what was and wasn't within your control? Journal your answers.

2.   What have you learned about moving beyond guilt and remorse as a result of this chapter? How does this compare to ways you have responded in the past? Journal your answers.

3.   What part of the healing process do you find most difficult? How will you overcome this? What resources will you add to make this most effective? Journal your answers.

4. What are some dangers of not acknowledging and working through your painful feelings? What are some of the benefits of it? Journal regarding the techniques you will implement for grieving.

5. Knowing who you can share your deepest emotions with is vital for your well-being. Who is a trusted loved one you can confide in for a personal loss? Who can you confide in for the loss of a pet? Journal the reasons you value these people.

6. Find ways to program these coping mechanisms into your "preprogram." More information about how to "Reprogram Your Pre-Program" is found in *Elevate Your Mind to Success, Success Is Ele-MENTAL*, and at www.DrJillFandrich.com.

7. How will you utilize these skills to help other hurting people? Journal your answers.

8. Who will you share this information with? Who will benefit most from it? Journal your answers.

9. Apply critical thinking to the information you learned. More about critical thinking is found in *Who Connects Your Dots?, Medically Speaking, Who Connects Your Dots?*, and *Students: Who Connects Your Dots?*

10. Practice the skills you learned daily. Journal and monitor your progress.

CHAPTER 6

CASE STUDY FIVE: "WEATHER" OR NOT

Sami and David spent months planning their dream outdoor wedding in a picturesque garden. They meticulously chose every detail, from the flowers to the seating arrangements, envisioning a perfect day under the open sky. They began to imagine this pictorial event starting a year earlier so everything would be perfect. When the time finally came, the guests slowly arrived, one after the other, and the anticipation for the big event grew as they enjoyed one more sunny and pleasant day before the exchange of vows was to be made. On the morning of the wedding, however, dark clouds rolled in, and it was apparent that the dream garden wedding was about to take an unexpected turn, which they had not considered. Soon, a torrential rainstorm began. They quickly realized the need to move the ceremony inside a nearby barn, with their guests helping to rearrange everything at the last minute.

As you know, the weather was the Missing Variable in the unfortunate case of the not-so-picturesque wedding. While there are predictions about the weather and weather "forecasts," they are not always accurate, and "pop-up" systems can occur. It is especially difficult to anticipate weather patterns for an event such as a wedding planned up to a year or two ahead of time, as reservations may be booked quickly.

Weather forecasts are generated using advanced computer models that analyze data such as atmospheric conditions, temperature trends, wind patterns, and more. The accuracy of weather forecasts can vary depending on the time frame being predicted. Some studies claim short-term forecasts, typically up to three days in advance, tend to be more accurate, with about 90% accuracy. Medium-term forecasts, up to seven days, are generally accurate about 80% of the time. Long-term forecasts beyond seven days are less reliable due to the complexity of weather systems and are accurate up to 60% of the time. Factors such as the availability of data, the sophistication of the models used, and the unpredictability of certain weather events can also impact the accuracy of forecasts. Weather forecasts have become reasonably accurate over the years due to advancements in technology and data collection. Yet, there is always a margin of error involved in predicting future weather conditions.

Since the weather is a Missing Variable you cannot predict and most definitely cannot control, it is important to consider this in your outdoor plans and any type of plan where you need a specific kind of weather condition. There are things you can do to help reduce anxiety at the thought of a "bad weather invasion" and set yourself up for a greater chance of a successful event.

Ways to plan an outdoor event considering the weather:

1. *Have a backup plan*: Always have a contingency plan in case of bad weather. This could involve booking an indoor venue nearby or having tents available on standby.

2. *Monitor the weather forecast*: Monitor the weather forecast closely leading up to the event. Based on the latest updates, be prepared to make any necessary adjustments.

3. *Communicate with attendees*: Keep your guests informed about the weather and any potential event plan changes. Provide guidance on what they should do in case of rain or extreme weather.

4. *Rent equipment*: Renting or borrowing equipment such as tents, umbrellas, or portable heaters or fans can help mitigate the impact of unpredictable weather.

5. *Flexible timeline*: Build flexibility into your event schedule to allow for last-minute changes if needed due to weather conditions. This may be difficult for an event such as a wedding, yet as the weather can vary, be willing to admit everything may not go just as planned—and that's okay! Embrace the unpredictable nature of the weather and allow it to guide your

plans with grace and flexibility. Imagine the possible memorable events. Sometimes, the sun may hide behind the clouds, or the rain may pour down unexpectedly, altering your outdoor adventures. Remember, adapting and adjusting your schedule when the weather decides to take control is okay. Instead of feeling disappointed, see it as an opportunity to explore new indoor activities or venues, connect with loved ones over a cozy movie night, or simply enjoy a moment of peace and relaxation indoors. By staying open-minded and flexible, you can turn a weather-induced change of plans into a chance to create precious memories and find joy in unexpected moments. So, let go of expectations, embrace the beauty of spontaneity, and make the most of whatever the weather brings your way. Remember, it's not about the destination but the journey, even if that journey takes a different path than planned. Imagine how memorable it could be!

6. *Insurance coverage*: Consider purchasing event insurance that includes coverage for weather-related cancellations or disruptions if available. Ensure peace of mind on your special day with comprehensive insurance coverage for weather-related events like weddings. Avoid letting unexpected storms or other natural disasters ruin your celebration. There are actually policies to protect your investment that include provisions for rescheduling, venue damage, and vendor cancellations due to inclement weather. From securing your outdoor ceremony against rain to safeguarding your reception from unforeseen disruptions, tailored insurance plans can offer financial protection and flexibility to help you navigate any weather-related challenges. With this peace of mind, you can focus on creating unforgettable memories while you handle the uncertainties, ensuring that nothing stands in the way of your happily ever after.

7. *Stay calm and adapt*: Finally, stay calm and be prepared to adapt on the day of the event if the weather takes a turn for the worse. When the weather disrupts your outdoor plans,

this is key to making the most of the situation. The weather can be unpredictable, but how you respond can make all the difference. Maintaining a composed demeanor and being flexible in your approach can turn a potentially disappointing situation into a new and unexpected adventure. Rather than letting frustration take over, take a deep breath and assess the situation. Perhaps a sudden rainstorm means you can enjoy a delightful picnic under a shelter, or a change in wind direction opens up new possibilities for exploration. Embracing the elements and adjusting your plans accordingly can lead to unique experiences and memorable moments you wouldn't have encountered otherwise. Remember, nature operates on its own schedule, and sometimes, it's best to go with the flow rather than fight against it. By staying calm, adapting to the circumstances, and keeping an open mind, you can transform a weather-related setback into an opportunity for spontaneity and discovery. So, next time the weather throws a curveball your way, embrace the challenge and see where it takes you.

Planning ahead and staying flexible are crucial when dealing with weather and outdoor events. By planning ahead, you can anticipate potential weather conditions and prepare accordingly, ensuring the safety and comfort of attendees or guests. This includes having a backup plan in case of inclement weather, such as indoor venue options or alternative activities. Staying flexible allows you to adapt to changing weather conditions and make necessary adjustments to the event schedule or activities. It also enables you to take advantage of unexpected opportunities that may arise due to weather changes, such as clearing skies for outdoor activities.

Being prepared and having a flexible mindset can help mitigate the impact of adverse weather conditions on outdoor events, ensuring a successful and enjoyable experience for all participants. Additionally, it demonstrates foresight and responsiveness, enhancing your ability to manage and oversee the event effectively. A combination of careful planning and adaptability is key to ensuring the success and resilience of outdoor events in the face of unpredictable weather.

A group of friends planned a beach picnic to celebrate a special occasion. As they arrived at the beach, dark clouds loomed overhead, and soon a heavy rainstorm began. Disappointed, they sought shelter under a nearby pavilion. Instead of letting the weather ruin their day, they decided to make the most of the situation. They started playing games, sharing stories, and laughing together. The rain made the air cool and refreshing, adding to the cozy atmosphere. As they enjoyed the simple pleasures of each other's company, they realized that the unexpected turn of events had brought them closer together. They ended up having a wonderful time despite the weather. The sound of the raindrops on the roof became a soothing background to their conversations. They even danced in the rain, embracing the spontaneity of the moment. By accepting the circumstances and staying positive, they turned what could have been a disaster into a truly memorable event that strengthened their bond and created lasting memories.

As the weather can be a Missing Variable due to its inability to be controlled, you are still able to make some contingencies and allow for enjoyment in outdoor events despite potential inconsistencies. You are in control of your responses. Instead of feeling discouraged, you can choose to embrace the changing conditions with a positive mindset. You realize the rain brings a refreshing coolness to the air, invigorating your senses. The pitter-patter of raindrops creates a soothing background melody, adding a touch of magic to the atmosphere. With a smile on your face, you adapt to the weather by donning a colorful umbrella and waterproof gear. You see others doing the same, their spirits undampened by the showers. As you make your way to the event, you can't help but feel a sense of camaraderie with fellow attendees. The weather may have altered your original plans, but it has also brought people together in a unique way. You arrive at the event rain-kissed and ready to make the most of the day. The weather may be unpredictable, but your positive mindset can shine through, turning a potentially gloomy situation into a memorable and uplifting experience.

Reflect:

1. Recall a situation where you were a part of an outdoor event, and the weather didn't cooperate with your expectations. Describe the different emotions you felt. How did you respond? What was within your control? Journal your answers.

2. What have you learned about weather contingencies as a result of this chapter? How does this compare to your thoughts in the past? Journal your answers.

3. What part of weather unpredictability do you find most challenging? How will you be more flexible in your future responses? What backup plans will you add in the future? Journal your answers.

4. What are some dangers of not having a backup plan when weather is a factor? What are some of the benefits of backup plans? Journal regarding the plans you will implement on an outdoor occasion.

5. Staying calm and being adaptable are important for your well-being. How can you remain calm in an unexpected weather-related situation? Who is your accountability partner for remaining calm under stressful conditions? Journal the reasons you value this person.

6. Find ways to program calmness, flexibility, adaptability, and a positive mindset into your "preprogram." More information about how to "Reprogram Your Pre-Program" is found in *Elevate Your Mind to Success, Success Is Ele-MENTAL*, and at www.DrJillFandrich.com.

7. How will you utilize these skills to help other people? Journal your answers.

8. Who will you share this information with? Who will benefit most from it? Journal your answers.

9. Apply critical thinking to the information you learned. More about critical thinking is found in *Who Connects Your Dots?*, *Medically Speaking, Who Connects Your Dots?*, and *Students: Who Connects Your Dots?*

10. Practice the skills you learned daily. Journal and monitor your progress.

CHAPTER 7

Case Study Six: Temperamental Traffic

While driving to an important meeting, I reviewed everything I needed to gather to present to the staff. I had just enough time for final preparations, and I anticipated everything would fall into place nicely. At least—everything that was in *my* control. I suddenly found myself stuck in unexpected traffic due to a severe accident up ahead. The flashing lights of emergency vehicles signaled the seriousness of the situation, causing a knot of worry to form in my stomach. I could feel the minutes ticking as the traffic came to a standstill, with no way around the accident. Frustration and impatience began to bubble up inside me as I realized I might miss my meeting. I tried to calm myself by taking deep breaths and reminding myself that my safety was more important than being on time. As the emergency crews worked to clear the scene, I couldn't help but feel a sense of empathy for those involved in the accident. It was a sobering reminder of how quickly life can change and how precious every moment truly is. Finally, after what felt like an eternity, the traffic started moving again. As I passed the accident site, I sent a silent prayer for the well-being of those affected. The experience left me feeling grateful for my own safety and determined to make the most of every moment I have.

While traffic patterns can be a variable, accidents are the Missing Variables in this case study. Traffic accidents are a common occurrence on roads worldwide, often resulting in injuries, fatalities, and damage to vehicles. Despite advancements in technology and safety regulations, the reality is that accidents are sometimes beyond human control. Factors such as weather conditions, mechanical failures, and unpredictable behaviors of other drivers can all contribute to the likelihood of an accident. In these situations, even the most cautious and skilled drivers may be unable to avoid a collision. As much as we strive to prevent accidents through defensive driving and adherence to traffic laws, some circumstances are simply out of our hands. It serves as a reminder of the unpredictability of the road and traffic and the importance of staying vigilant and prepared at all times while behind the wheel.

As a driver, you *do* have control over several key elements of driving safety. By practicing defensive driving techniques, maintaining your vehicle properly, and adhering to traffic laws, you can significantly reduce the risk of accidents on the road. Your focus, alertness, and decision-making behind the wheel play a crucial role in ensuring your safety and the safety of others. Avoiding distractions like texting, speeding, and driving under the influence are all within your control and can greatly improve your ability to react to unexpected situations. Safe driving is a responsibility that rests in your hands, and by staying vigilant and proactive, you can help create a safer environment for everyone on the road.

Knowing that traffic patterns can be inconsistent and accidents can be beyond your control, it is important to consider these things as you prepare to drive in traffic. It is also essential to consider these things when you have an important, timely event to attend.

What to consider regarding traffic as you plan to attend an important meeting:

1. *Traffic patterns*: Understand the typical traffic patterns for the route you will be taking around the time of your meeting. Check for any known congestion points or road closures.

2. *Alternative routes*: Identify alternative routes in case your primary route is congested or blocked. Navigation apps can help you find the fastest route based on real-time traffic data.

3. *Departure time*: Allow ample time to account for potential delays. Consider leaving early to buffer against unexpected traffic jams or accidents.

4. *Public transportation*: Evaluate whether taking public transportation, such as trains or buses, could be a more reliable option to navigate traffic.

5. *Parking availability*: If driving, research parking options near the meeting location in advance to avoid wasting time searching for a spot.

6. *Communication*: Have necessary contact information handy and inform the meeting organizers if you encounter unexpected delays due to traffic to manage expectations and adjust schedules if appropriate. By considering these factors and planning ahead, you can minimize the impact of traffic on your journey to the important meeting.

7. *Meeting schedule*: If there are concerns about the unpredictability of traffic, schedule meetings during the day while you are already in attendance, if possible. For example, if this is a work meeting, schedule the event for mid-morning or afternoon if you live in a congested area and have input into scheduling.

Tess had an important meeting scheduled, and as she headed out the door, she noticed heavy traffic on her usual route. Instead of panicking, she quickly checked her GPS and found an alternative route that seemed clear. Trusting her instincts, Tess took the detour despite being unfamiliar with the new path. As she drove down winding roads and through unfamiliar neighborhoods, Tess remained calm and focused. She reminded herself that being prepared for unexpected delays was part of her job. As she neared the meeting location, she saw the main road she had avoided was now at a standstill due to a major accident. Thanks to her quick thinking and adaptability, Tess arrived at the meeting with plenty of time to spare. She even had a moment to collect her thoughts and review her notes before the others arrived. The meeting was a success, and Tess's colleagues were impressed by her punctuality and composure. From that day on, Tess made it a habit always to have a backup plan and remain flexible in the face of obstacles. She learned that sometimes, taking a different path can lead to even greater success.

Leaving early when traveling to an important meeting or event is crucial to ensure punctuality and preparedness. You can mitigate the risk of arriving late and missing out on valuable opportunities by allowing extra time for unexpected delays, such as traffic, unforeseen circumstances, or transportation issues. Being early also allows for a sense of calmness and collectedness, enabling you to gather your thoughts, review important information, and enter the meeting or event with confidence. Arriving early demonstrates respect for others' time and reflects professionalism and reliability. It sets a positive tone for the meeting or event and shows a commitment to being organized and on top of your responsibilities. In general, the habit of leaving early not only helps you avoid unnecessary stress but also positions you for success by starting off on the right foot.

Staying calm when stuck in traffic is crucial for maintaining your mental well-being and safety on the road. Keeping a level head can help reduce stress and frustration, leading to a more positive driving experience. It also allows you to make better decisions and react more effectively to unexpected situations. By practicing patience and mindfulness, you can turn a potentially frustrating situation into an opportunity to relax, listen to music or audiobooks, or catch up on a podcast. Remember, getting upset won't make the traffic move any faster, so take a deep breath, stay patient, and focus on arriving at your destination safely.

Ways to stay calm when stuck in traffic:

1. Listen to calming music, audiobooks, or podcasts to help distract you from the traffic situation and learn in the process.

2. Practice deep breathing exercises to help lower stress levels and promote relaxation.

3. Use the time to catch up on phone calls with friends or family members.

4. Have a notepad with you and jot down notes or ideas of things that come to mind.

5. Plan ahead by leaving earlier or finding alternate routes to avoid future traffic jams.

6. Keep a bottle of water and healthy snacks in the car to stay hydrated and nourished.

7. Use the opportunity to practice mindfulness by focusing on the present moment and accepting the situation without judgment.

8. Play games or puzzles on your phone to keep your mind engaged and distracted from the traffic (when not moving!)

9. Take the time to appreciate the surroundings by observing nature or buildings around you.

10. Use voice assistants to keep informed of the latest news updates or weather forecasts.

11. Consider learning a new skill or language through audio lessons to make productive use of your time while waiting in traffic.

Patience is a virtue that holds immense value in our fast-paced world. Developing the character quality of patience is crucial for fostering resilience, understanding, and empathy. In a society that often values instant gratification, patience allows you to persevere through challenges and setbacks with grace and composure. It teaches you to wait for the right moment, listen attentively, and approach situations calmly and rationally. Patience enables you to build stronger relationships, make better decisions, and achieve long-term goals. By cultivating patience, you learn the power of self-control and the ability to adapt to unexpected circumstances with a positive attitude. Through patience, you can truly appreciate the journey and savor the rewards of your efforts. In a world where everything moves rapidly, patience becomes a precious quality that not only benefits you individually but also contributes to a more compassionate and understanding society. So, how can you develop more patience?

Ways to develop the character quality of patience:

1. *Practicing mindfulness*: Being present in the moment can help cultivate patience by teaching you to accept things as they are without reacting impulsively.

2. *Cultivating gratitude*: Focusing on what you are grateful for can shift the perspective from impatience to appreciation, helping to build patience over time.

3. *Setting realistic goals*: Breaking down large tasks into smaller ones can help in managing expectations and prevent frustration, leading to a more patient approach.

4. *Practicing empathy*: Understanding others' perspectives and situations can increase tolerance and patience in challenging interactions.

5. *Learning to manage stress*: Developing stress management techniques can prevent impatience from escalating under challenging situations. Learn effective ways to calm yourself.

6. *Have a backup activity*: Keeping yourself busy can distract your mind from stress and chaos. Having a plan for activities to occupy your mind can be helpful. Keep a book or crossword puzzle with you at all times to read. Keep a notepad nearby to jot down ideas, thoughts, or even a grocery list. Bring a micro recorder or use your phone to record your to-do list. Be creative and use your time wisely.

7. *Engaging in activities that promote patience*: Activities like meditation, praying, puzzling, or deep breathing exercises can help in developing a more patient mindset.

8. *Seeking support*: Surrounding yourself with patient people or seeking guidance from mentors can provide positive examples and encouragement for personal growth in patience. By incorporating these strategies into daily life, you can gradually enhance your capacity for patience and cultivate a more resilient and understanding character.

9. *Pray for patience*: When you pray for patience, you are asking for inner strength to endure challenges, setbacks, and difficult circumstances without losing your composure. Patience allows you to maintain a sense of calm and understanding in the face of adversity, helping you navigate through life's trials with

grace and resilience. Praying for patience can lead to personal growth and development as you learn to accept things as they are, practice empathy toward others, and trust in the process of life. It can also help you cultivate a more positive outlook, reduce stress and anxiety, and improve your relationships with others. However—it is worth noting that building patience often involves facing situations that test your resolve and perseverance. So, when you pray for patience, *be prepared* to encounter challenges that will help you develop this virtue over time. Trust in the process, stay committed to your intentions and remember that patience is a valuable trait that can lead to greater peace and understanding in your life.

Ian sat in his car, staring at the sea of brake lights ahead. He checked his watch anxiously, knowing he was already running late for an important meeting. Despite the honking horns and frustrated drivers around him, Ian decided to practice patience. Instead of getting agitated, he focused on breathing and remained calm. He turned up the radio, enjoying the music and the chance to unwind amidst the chaos. As the minutes ticked by, he reminded himself that getting upset wouldn't make the traffic move any faster. Ian used the extra time to go over his presentation in his head, making sure he was well-prepared for the meeting. He even took a moment to appreciate the sunset, painting the sky in hues of orange and pink. Finally, after what seemed like an eternity, the traffic began to move. Ian arrived at his meeting just in time, feeling surprisingly relaxed and ready to tackle whatever challenges came his way. Through patience and a positive attitude, Ian turned what could have been a stressful situation into a moment of tranquility and productivity.

Empathy toward the hurting accident victim was mentioned in a previous case study. It is important to think of others and what they are experiencing. Empathy is a powerful tool that allows you to connect with others on a deeper level, understanding their feelings and perspectives with compassion and kindness. Practicing empathy fosters stronger relationships, promotes understanding, and creates a more inclusive and supportive community. It helps you to communicate better, resolve conflicts peacefully, and build trust with those around you. Empathy enables you to walk in someone else's shoes, offering comfort and encouragement during challenging times and celebrating their successes with genuine joy. It is a fundamental building block of emotional intelligence and plays a crucial role in promoting mental well-being and a sense of belonging. By showing empathy toward others, you not only enhance your own emotional intelligence but also contribute to a more compassionate and harmonious society where everyone feels valued and understood.

Ways to display empathy toward others:

1. *Practice active listening:* Give your full attention when someone is speaking, maintain eye contact, and avoid interrupting.

2. *Show understanding:* Acknowledge the other person's feelings and perspective without judgment. Use phrases like "I understand how you feel" or "That must be difficult for you." Or even, "Help me understand how you feel."

3. *Validate their emotions:* Let the person know their feelings are valid and important. Offer words of comfort and reassurance.

4. *Offer support:* Ask how you can help, whether through practical assistance or simply being there to listen. Show that you care and are willing to provide assistance.

5. *Be present:* Show empathy through your body language and tone of voice. Offer a comforting touch or a warm smile to demonstrate your support.

6. *Avoid giving unsolicited advice:* Instead of immediately offering solutions, focus on understanding the person's emotions and providing a listening ear. By practicing these behaviors, you can create a safe and supportive environment where others feel heard, understood, and valued.

7. *Pray for them:* Praying for someone is a powerful act of empathy, transcending distance and barriers to connect with the thoughts and emotions of another. In offering prayers for someone, you step into their world, seeking to understand their struggles, joys, and desires. Through prayer, you express care,

compassion, and solidarity, creating a bridge of understanding and support. It is a selfless gesture that reflects your capacity to empathize with others, recognizing their humanity and interconnectedness with your own. Whether in times of joy, sorrow, or uncertainty, praying for someone is an expression of love and empathy that can uplift spirits, provide comfort, and strengthen bonds. It is a reminder of your shared humanity and the power of connection that transcends words and actions. As you hold someone in your thoughts and prayers, you offer them a piece of your heart, knowing that in doing so, you cultivate empathy, understanding, and a sense of unity in the world.

Proper preparation is crucial for a safe and timely journey to an important event. Planning ahead allows for adequate time to consider all factors that may affect the trip, from weather conditions to traffic patterns. Checking the route, assessing potential risks, and ensuring the vehicle is in good working condition are key elements of preparation. Packing essentials, such as identification documents, emergency supplies, and necessary items for the event, is also important. Additionally, having a backup plan in case of unexpected circumstances can help mitigate potential delays. By taking the time to prepare thoroughly, you can increase the likelihood of reaching your destination safely and on time, minimizing stress and maximizing enjoyment of the event.

 Reflect:

1. Recall a situation where you had an important event to attend, and traffic conditions or an accident caused a delay. Describe how this affected you. Describe how you felt. How did you respond? Journal your answers.

2. What have you learned about traffic contingencies as a result of this chapter? How does this compare to your thoughts in the past? Journal your answers.

3. What part of the traffic unpredictability do you find most challenging? How will you be more flexible in your future responses? What preparation backup plans will you add in the future? Journal your answers.

4. What are some dangers of not having a backup plan when traffic is a factor? What are some of the benefits of extra preparations? Journal regarding the plans you will implement for the next important meeting you must travel to.

5. Staying calm and being adaptable is important for your well-being. How can you remain calm in a tense traffic-related situation? Who is your accountability partner for remaining calm under stressful conditions? Journal the reasons you value this person.

6. Find ways to program calmness, patience, adaptability, and empathy into your "preprogram." More information about how to "Reprogram Your Pre-Program" is found in *Elevate Your Mind to Success*, *Success Is Ele-MENTAL*, and at www.DrJillFandrich.com.

7. How will you utilize these skills to help other people? Journal your answers.

8. Who will you share this information with? Who will benefit most from it? Journal your answers.

9. Apply critical thinking to the information you learned. More about critical thinking is found in *Who Connects Your Dots?*, *Medically Speaking, Who Connects Your Dots?*, and *Students: Who Connects Your Dots?*

10. Practice the skills you learned daily. Journal and monitor your progress.

CHAPTER 8

CASE STUDY SEVEN: TROUBLING TREATMENT

In a bustling school, there was a bright student named Lily. Despite her eagerness to learn, she often found herself being mistreated by her classmates. They teased her about her love for books and mocked her quiet demeanor. Lily tried to ignore the hurtful remarks, but the words stung like daggers. As days went by, the mistreatment intensified. Lily felt alone and powerless, unable to control the actions of others. She confided in her teachers, who tried to address the issue, but the bullying persisted. Lily's grades began to suffer, and her once vibrant spirit started to fade.

Navigating life with inconsiderate people can be challenging, as their actions and attitudes can greatly impact your own well-being. It can be frustrating and disheartening to deal with people who seem oblivious to your feelings and needs. However, it's important to remember that you cannot control the behavior of others. You can only control how you react and respond to the situation. Practicing patience, setting boundaries, and focusing on self-care are essential strategies for managing interactions with inconsiderate people. While it may be difficult, finding ways to maintain your own peace of mind and emotional balance in the midst of such circumstances is key to preserving your own happiness and mental health. Remember, you are not responsible for the actions of others, but you do have the power to choose how you let them affect you.

Understanding that you can only control your own response and actions, rather than trying to control others, is a crucial realization in achieving personal growth and healthy relationships. By focusing on how you choose to react to situations and people, you empower yourself to maintain inner peace and strength, regardless of external circumstances. This mindset shift allows you to let go of unnecessary stress and anxiety caused by trying to influence or change others, leading to a more fulfilling and harmonious life. Embracing the principle of controlling only what is within your power ultimately fosters self-awareness, resilience, and emotional intelligence. It enables you to navigate challenges gracefully, communicate effectively, and cultivate authentic connections based on understanding and respect. Remember, the power lies in how *you choose* to respond, not in trying to dictate the actions of others.

In a world where we often encounter negativity and mistreatment from others, it becomes crucial to remember the importance of being patient and caring with yourself. It is easy to internalize the hurtful actions of others, which could be in a school, a business, or within your own friends or family unit, but you must realize that you cannot control how others choose to treat you. Instead, you can control how you respond and care for yourself in such situations. Practicing self-compassion and patience during challenging times can help you maintain your mental and emotional well-being. By showing yourself kindness and understanding, you build resilience and inner strength to navigate difficult circumstances. It is not a reflection of your worth when others mistreat you, but rather a reflection of their own struggles and insecurities. By prioritizing self-care and compassion, you empower yourself to rise above negativity and cultivate a positive relationship with yourself. Embracing patience and self-love allows you to protect your peace and maintain a healthy mindset, regardless of the actions of others. So, be gentle with yourself, practice self-compassion, and remember that you deserve kindness, especially from yourself.

People may choose to treat others poorly due to a variety of reasons. One of the main reasons is a lack of empathy or consideration for others, which can lead to selfish or malicious behavior. Insecurities and low self-esteem can also drive people to belittle or mistreat others in an attempt to feel superior or deflect attention from *their* own shortcomings. Additionally, past negative experiences or trauma can cause them to lash out at others as a way to cope with their own pain or anger. Social influences, such as peer pressure or cultural norms that condone aggression or discrimination, can also play a role in why people choose to treat others poorly. Some people may simply lack the necessary emotional intelligence or coping skills to navigate conflicts or challenging situations constructively, leading them to resort to negative behaviors.

When people have deep-seated insecurities, they often struggle with feelings of inadequacy, fear, and self-doubt. These insecurities can manifest in negative ways, leading them to project their own issues onto others through mistreatment or harmful behavior. For example, a person who feels insecure about his intelligence may try to belittle others in an attempt to feel superior. Someone insecure about her appearance may criticize or bully others to deflect attention away from her own perceived flaws. Insecurities can also breed jealousy, causing people to undermine or sabotage those they perceive as threats.

By putting others down, these people may temporarily alleviate their own insecurities by asserting dominance or control. However, this behavior is often a maladaptive coping mechanism that can perpetuate a cycle of negativity and harm both themselves and those around them. It is important to remember that while insecurities can contribute to someone treating others poorly, it is not an excuse for harmful behavior. This is a problem with the other person, not you. Encouraging self-awareness and empathy and seeking professional help can help them address their insecurities in a healthier way and foster more positive relationships.

In a world where mistreatment can be a harsh reality, it is crucial to prioritize self-care when someone is wrongly treating you. When faced with unjust treatment from others, it is essential to remember that you deserve kindness and respect. By focusing on your own well-being and self-worth, you can protect yourself from the negative impact of such behavior. Embracing self-care practices such as setting boundaries, practicing self-compassion, and seeking support can empower you to navigate challenging situations with strength and resilience. Remember, your worth is not defined by how others treat you but by how you choose to care for yourself in the face of adversity. So, prioritize your self-care, stand up for your boundaries, and remember that you are worthy of love and respect, no matter how others may try to mistreat you.

Things you can focus on when someone is wrongly treating you:

1. Take a deep breath and stay calm to avoid reacting impulsively.

2. Clarify the situation by asking questions to understand their perspective.

3. Assertively communicate your feelings and boundaries without aggression.

4. Practice empathy by trying to see things from their point of view.

5. Focus on other people who might be in need of some help. The diversion can prove to be rewarding.

6. Focus on gratitude and appreciating people in your life and the things you have and can do.

7. Set boundaries and clearly communicate what behavior is unacceptable to you.

8. Seek support from friends, family, or a therapist to process your emotions.

9. Focus on your self-worth and remind yourself that you deserve respect.

10. Consider the other person's intentions and whether the behavior was intentional or unintentional. If they intentionally try to hurt you, understand that is a weakness and insecurity in them, not you.

11. Reflect on how you can constructively assert yourself to address the situation.

12. Remember that you cannot control others' actions, but you can control how you respond to them.

13. Focus on your own personal growth and success.

One day, during a particularly harsh encounter with her classmates, Lily made a decision. Instead of succumbing to the negativity, she chose to focus on her own growth and well-being. She immersed herself in her studies, finding solace in the pages of her favorite books. Despite the ongoing mistreatment, Lily remained resilient. She realized that she couldn't control the actions of others, but she could control how she responded to them. With newfound strength and determination, Lily faced each day with courage, knowing that the words of others did not define her worth.

Like Lily, you are worth spending time developing and growing. You can do many things to build your confidence and sense of self-worth. It is important to understand that these are things you can control.

Ways to build your self-confidence and self-worth:

1. *Practice self-care:* As previously mentioned, take care of your physical, emotional, and mental well-being through activities like exercise, meditation, and hobbies you enjoy. Take a detox bath and energize yourself.

2. *Set realistic goals:* Break down larger goals into smaller, achievable steps to build a sense of accomplishment and boost confidence.

3. *Challenge negative self-talk:* Replace self-critical thoughts with positive affirmations and focus on your strengths and successes.

4. *Surround yourself with positive influences:* Spend time with supportive and encouraging people who uplift you and believe in your abilities.

5. *Learn and grow:* Continuously seek personal and professional development opportunities to enhance your skills and knowledge. Embracing self-growth and continuous learning is a powerful journey that can profoundly impact your confidence and self-worth. By investing time and effort in personal development, you can discover your strengths, overcome limitations, and unleash your full potential. You gain a deeper understanding of yourself through self-reflection and introspection, building a strong foundation for confidence to flourish. As you acquire new skills, knowledge, and experiences, you expand your comfort

zone and challenge your perceived limitations. This growth process fosters a sense of achievement and empowerment, reinforcing a positive self-image and boosting self-esteem. The pursuit of self-improvement cultivates resilience and adaptability, enabling you to navigate challenges with grace and confidence. As you embrace lifelong learning and personal growth, you become more self-assured, resilient, and capable of overcoming obstacles. Ultimately, focusing on self-growth not only enhances your skills and abilities but also nourishes a sense of worthiness and self-assurance that radiates from within.

6.   *Celebrate your achievements*: Acknowledge and celebrate your accomplishments, no matter how small, to reinforce a positive self-image. This will help you recall your strengths and build more confidence.

7.   *Practice gratitude*: Reflect on the things you are grateful for in your life to cultivate a mindset of abundance and positivity. Practicing gratitude is a powerful tool that can significantly boost confidence and self-worth. By acknowledging and appreciating the positive aspects of life, you can shift your focus away from shortcomings and insecurities toward your strengths and blessings. This shift in perspective helps cultivate a sense of self-assurance and worthiness as you begin to recognize your own value and capabilities. Regularly expressing gratitude can also lead to increased feelings of contentment and satisfaction, reinforcing a positive self-image. As you become more attuned to the abundance in your life, you develop a deeper sense of inner peace and fulfillment, bolstering your confidence in navigating life's challenges. Furthermore, gratitude fosters a sense of resilience and optimism, helping you approach setbacks and obstacles with a more positive outlook. By acknowledging and being thankful for the support, opportunities, and achievements in your life, you can build a strong foundation of self-belief and empowerment that propels you toward further growth and success. In essence, gratitude

serves as a catalyst for enhancing confidence and self-worth, enabling you to embrace your true potential and thrive in all aspects of life.

8. *Seek help if needed*: If you struggle with low self-confidence or self-worth, don't hesitate to seek support from a therapist or counselor.

9. *Pray*: Prayer is a powerful tool that can significantly impact your confidence and self-worth. By connecting with God through prayer, you can find a sense of inner peace, strength, and guidance. This spiritual practice can help you cultivate a positive mindset, overcome self-doubt, and boost your self-esteem. Through prayer, you can feel a sense of purpose, belonging, and worthiness, knowing you are supported and loved *unconditionally*. It provides a space for reflection, gratitude, and self-acceptance, allowing you to let go of your insecurities and embrace your true self. By surrendering your worries and fears to your Heavenly Father, you can experience a profound sense of empowerment and confidence in your God-given abilities to navigate life's challenges. Prayer can serve as a source of encouragement, inspiration, and reassurance, helping you believe in yourself and your potential. Prayer can foster a deep sense of self-worth and confidence that transcends external validation and empowers you to live authentically and passionately.

10. *Pray for your offender*: Praying *for your offender* can boost your confidence and self-worth by shifting your focus from bitterness and anger toward empathy and forgiveness. When you pray for someone who has wronged you, you are choosing to let go of negative emotions and instead channel positive energy toward them. This act of compassion and understanding can help you feel more in control of your emotions and reactions. Additionally, praying for your offender can provide a sense of inner peace and strength, knowing that you are taking the higher road and choosing to respond with grace and kindness. This can boost your self-worth by reinforcing your values and integrity.

By praying for your offender, you are practicing empathy and understanding, which can enhance your emotional insight and ability to handle difficult situations with grace. This can, in turn, boost your confidence in your ability to navigate challenging relationships and conflicts. Praying for your offender can help you let go of negativity, cultivate empathy and forgiveness, and strengthen your sense of self-worth and confidence in handling difficult situations with grace.

While it is important not to respond with harmful revenge, there is a type of revenge that will always be to your benefit without physically harming anyone else. Choosing not to seek revenge doesn't mean allowing yourself to be a doormat. When others try to bring you down, use that negativity to fuel your success. Let your accomplishments speak louder than any petty actions taken against you. Rise above the negativity and focus on building the life you want. Show them that their attempts to hurt you only made you stronger. Your success becomes the ultimate revenge, proving that you are resilient and unwavering in the face of adversity. There is no need for retaliation when you can let your achievements do the talking. Keep pushing forward, and let the naysayers watch in awe as you continue to thrive despite their efforts to bring you down. Your goal isn't even to prove anything to them but rather to use the harmful intentions to your advantage for personal growth. If and when they happen to notice your progress, it is just an added bonus.

Focusing on what you can control can enhance resilience against the hurtfulness of others by shifting the attention toward actionable steps that empower you. By directing energy toward aspects within your control, such as reactions, boundaries, and self-care, you can cultivate a sense of agency and reduce the impact of external negativity. This proactive approach enables you to choose how to respond to hurtful situations, fostering emotional strength and adaptive coping strategies. Emphasizing personal control also encourages self-reflection and growth, promoting resilience in the face of adversity. By recognizing and accepting the limitations of what you can influence, you can develop a mindset that is less vulnerable to the opinions and actions of others, ultimately building inner strength and emotional well-being. In essence, focusing on what you can control serves as a powerful tool for navigating challenging interactions and fostering resilience in the face of hurtfulness.

In a world where cruelty lurks in the shadows, one truth remains crystal clear: you cannot tame the vicious hearts of those who seek to harm you. No matter how hard you try, their words may cut, and their actions may wound, but one power they can never take away from you is the strength to choose your own response. Like a mighty oak weathering the storm, you stand tall in the face of adversity. You are the master of your emotions, the architect of your fate. When the darkness beckons, you shine brighter with resilience and grace, refusing to let the venom of others poison your spirit. For in the end, it is not the cruelty of others that defines you, but how you rise above it with unwavering dignity and unwavering resolve. So, let their arrows fly, let their daggers strike, for you are a warrior forged in the fires of adversity, unbreakable and unyielding. Remember this: you may not control their actions, but you hold the key to your own liberation.

 Reflect:

1. Recall a situation where others mistreated you. Describe how this affected you. Describe how you felt. How did you respond? What would you do differently? Journal your answers.

2. What have you learned about handling hurtful situations as a result of this chapter? How does this compare to your responses in the past? Journal your answers.

3. What part of the suggested responses do you find most challenging? How will you choose to respond in the future to an unfortunate, hurtful occurrence? What can you do to build your confidence and self-worth now? Journal your answers.

4. What are some dangers of not being prepared for "troubling treatment?" What are some of the benefits of setting boundaries? Journal regarding the boundaries you will implement.

5. Developing a positive mindset is important for your well-being. How can you cultivate positivity in a hurtful situation? Who is your accountability partner for venting in hurtful conditions such as this? Journal the reasons you value this person.

6. Find ways to program resilience, self-confidence, and inner peace into your "preprogram." More information about how to "Reprogram Your Pre-Program" is found in *Elevate Your Mind to Success*, *Success Is Ele-MENTAL*, and at www.DrJillFandrich.com.

7. How will you utilize these skills to help other people? Journal your answers.

8. Who will you share this information with? Who will benefit most from it? Journal your answers.

9. Apply critical thinking to the information you learned. More about critical thinking is found in *Who Connects Your Dots?*, *Medically Speaking, Who Connects Your Dots?*, and *Students: Who Connects Your Dots?*

10. Practice the skills you learned daily. Journal and monitor your progress.

CHAPTER 9

CASE STUDY EIGHT: IMPLODING INSTRUCTIONS

Alex was tasked with crafting a beautiful wooden chair by his mentor, Master Carpenter Thomas. Eager to impress, Alex diligently followed each instruction to the letter, measuring twice and cutting once. After weeks of meticulous work, the chair was finally completed. However, when Thomas came to inspect the final product, he was puzzled. Though structurally sound, the chair bore little resemblance to the elegant design he had envisioned. Confused and disappointed, Alex asked where he went wrong despite following instructions precisely. Thomas explained that while Alex had indeed followed the instructions perfectly, he had missed an important step—using his creativity and intuition to bring the design to life.

In this case study, the Missing Variables were creativity and intuition despite following the instructions meticulously. They were Missing Variables because they couldn't have been known to Alex unless Thomas had revealed them to him. They were out of his control. Have you ever worked with a set of instructions or even a recipe where you followed them exactly, yet the result was not what you or the one you were preparing it for expected? For example, you followed a recipe to the last teaspoon, yet the bread was doughy in the middle or crisp on the bottom. What other factors could be Missing Variables? Elevation? Oven wattage?

What if you were to create a beautiful and complete product but didn't even have all of the instructions? How do you finalize the project in this example without all the pieces? In this case, the Missing Variable is the missing information!

Creating something perfectly from instructions can be a daunting task, especially when crucial pieces of the puzzle are missing. Like trying to complete a jigsaw puzzle without all the pieces, there's a sense of frustration and uncertainty that comes with not having the whole picture. You may follow the steps meticulously, but achieving the desired outcome without all the necessary information becomes challenging. It's akin to assembling a complex machine with some components still undiscovered or understanding a story with key chapters torn out. The end result may still be functional or coherent to an extent, but the perfection you strive for remains just out of reach. Each missing piece represents a gap in knowledge or understanding that hinders your ability to bring everything together flawlessly. This struggle highlights the importance of thorough preparation and clear communication to ensure all necessary elements are available. It also emphasizes the value of adaptability and problem-solving skills when faced with incomplete instructions. Ultimately, the journey to perfection is not just about following directions but also about addressing the unknowns and finding creative solutions or using innovation to fill in the gaps.

You may not always have all the necessary information, even with a complete set of instructions or recipes. You can ask clarifying questions to determine if more information is needed. You can also analyze the context of the conversation or document to see if there are any gaps in the information provided. Use critical thinking. Additionally, look for keywords or phrases that typically indicate a need for more information, such as "I don't understand" or "Can you explain further?"

Find related topics or offer examples to prompt the end recipient to provide more details. If necessary, politely request the user to elaborate on their question or concern. Through these methods, you can effectively gauge whether additional information is required to provide a satisfactory response. However, there will always be times when you don't know what you don't know!

Realizing the value of artistic expression in craftsmanship, Alex set out to redesign the chair, incorporating his own unique touches. The result was a stunning masterpiece that surpassed even Thomas' expectations. From then on, Alex learned that while following instructions was important, sometimes it was equally crucial to trust his own instincts and inject a bit of personal flair into the process.

Intuition is the ability to understand or know something without conscious reasoning. It is often described as a gut feeling or intuitive understanding of a situation. In cases where you don't have all the necessary information, intuition can be a valuable tool to guide decision-making. When faced with incomplete information, intuition can help fill the gaps by drawing on past experiences, patterns, and subconscious cues. It can provide insights that may not be immediately apparent through logical analysis. By tapping into your intuition, you can make quicker decisions and confidently navigate complex situations.

To use intuition effectively in such cases, it is important to cultivate self-awareness and trust in your instincts. This can be done through practices such as mindfulness, meditation, critical thinking, and reflection on past experiences. Balancing intuition with rational thinking is essential to ensure sound decision-making. Ultimately, intuition can serve as a valuable complement to analytical thinking, especially when time is limited or information is scarce. You can enhance your problem-solving skills and make more informed choices despite uncertainty by honing your intuitive abilities and critical thinking skills. Improving intuition skills involves honing your ability to understand and interpret subtle cues and patterns. It is a process that takes time and practice to develop. Be patient as you work to enhance this skill.

Ways to improve intuition skills:

1. *Practice mindfulness:* By staying present in the moment, you can better tune in to your instincts and gut feelings.

2. *Trust your instincts:* Start by acknowledging and listening to your intuition, even if it initially seems irrational. Be confident and learn to trust yourself.

3. *Awareness:* Awareness is a fundamental character quality that can significantly improve intuition. By being attuned to your surroundings, emotions, and thoughts, you develop a heightened sense of perception and insight. This increased awareness allows you to pick up on subtle cues, patterns, and energies that may not be immediately apparent. As a result,

you can make more informed decisions, anticipate outcomes, and navigate challenges with greater clarity and confidence. Cultivating awareness enables you to understand yourself and others better, fostering empathy, emotional intelligence, and deeper connections. By being in tune with your own emotions and motivations, you can better interpret your intuition and gut feelings, leading to more authentic and aligned actions. In essence, awareness serves as a foundation for honing intuition by sharpening your ability to observe, interpret, and respond to the world around you. By developing this character quality, you can tap into your inner wisdom and intuition, allowing you to navigate life's complexities with grace and insight.

4. *Journaling*: Keeping a journal of your intuitive thoughts and feelings can help you track patterns and enhance self-awareness. Review your journals routinely and learn from past excerpts.

5. *Meditation*: Meditation can help quiet the mind, increase self-awareness, and strengthen intuition.

6. *Engage in creative activities*: Activities like painting, writing, "puzzling," or music can help tap into your intuitive side and foster creativity.

7. *Past experiences*: Learn from past experiences by observing outcomes. This can develop intuitive thoughts about potential future results.

8. *Listen to your body*: Pay attention to physical sensations that may signal your intuition at work, such as feelings of unease or excitement.

9. *Seek feedback*: Discussing your intuitive insights with others can provide valuable feedback and help validate your instincts.

Critical thinking is analyzing, evaluating, and interpreting information to make informed decisions or judgments. It involves being objective, logical, and reflective in order to identify biases, assumptions, and logical fallacies that may influence thinking. You can effectively assess arguments, evidence, and information by applying critical thinking skills to reach well-reasoned conclusions.

When it comes to intuition, critical thinking can help increase its effectiveness by providing a framework for evaluating and validating intuitive insights. By critically examining the underlying reasons and evidence supporting an intuitive feeling, you can ensure that your intuition is not simply based on biases or wishful thinking. Critical thinking can also help recognize when intuition may be useful and when it may lead to erroneous conclusions.

Combining critical thinking with intuition allows you to make more informed and rational decisions by leveraging both analytical reasoning and intuitive insights. By questioning assumptions, seeking evidence, and considering alternative perspectives, critical thinking can enhance the accuracy and reliability of intuitive judgments, leading to better outcomes in various situations.

Critical thinking is a valuable skill that can enhance any project, even when detailed instructions are provided. By applying critical thinking, you can analyze information, identify potential gaps or errors in the instructions, and make informed decisions to improve the project's execution. Even with a complete set of instructions, critical thinking allows you to anticipate challenges, consider alternative approaches, and adapt to unforeseen circumstances. It enables you to evaluate the instructions critically, ensuring they are logical, accurate, and feasible.

Critical thinking can help uncover hidden opportunities for innovation or efficiency that may not be apparent in the instructions. It promotes accountability and ownership of the project. By questioning assumptions, clarifying objectives, and assessing risks, you can proactively address potential issues before they escalate. This approach fosters a sense of responsibility and empowers you to make effective decisions contributing to the project's success. Critical thinking is a powerful tool that *complements* a full set of instructions by enabling you to engage thoughtfully, problem-solve creatively, and achieve optimal outcomes. It encourages a mindset of continuous improvement and adaptability, essential qualities for navigating complex projects successfully.

Della and Max purchased a toy for their child, Mia. The instructions provided were complex and confusing, leaving them feeling frustrated.

Instead of giving up, they relied on their intuition and critical thinking skills. They carefully examined each piece, discussing how they could fit together based on their understanding of mechanics. They used their creativity to come up with alternative ways to assemble the toy when the instructions failed them. Despite facing challenges along the way, they remained patient and determined. Through trial and error, Della and Max slowly pieced the toy together, drawing on their problem-solving abilities. They encouraged each other and celebrated small victories, knowing their effort would bring joy to Mia. Eventually, after many hours of hard work and perseverance, Della and Max successfully completed the build. Mia's eyes lit up with delight when she saw the finished product, and she couldn't wait to play with it. As they watched Mia happily play with her new toy, Della and Max realized that sometimes, intuition and critical thinking can lead to better outcomes than following complex and, therefore, inadequate instructions.

Ways to improve critical thinking skills:

1. Practice active listening to understand others' perspectives better.

2. Engage in debates or discussions to challenge your own beliefs and assumptions.

3. Read diverse sources of information to broaden your knowledge base.

4. Ask questions to clarify information and dig deeper into complex issues.

5. Evaluate evidence and sources critically for credibility and bias.

6. Practice problem-solving by breaking down complex issues into manageable parts.

7. Consider multiple viewpoints before forming conclusions.

8. Reflect on your own thinking process and identify areas for improvement.

9. Challenge yourself to think beyond your comfort zone.

10. Seek feedback from others to gain different perspectives on your thought process.

11. Read *Who Connects Your Dots?* or *Students: Who Connects Your Dots?*

As mentioned previously, awareness is a character quality that involves being conscious and perceptive of yourself, others, and your surroundings. It involves being mindful of what is happening both internally and externally, including thoughts, feelings, and actions. Awareness allows you to make informed decisions, understand the impact of your behavior on others, and navigate complex situations effectively. It also involves being open to new ideas, perspectives, and experiences, as well as being able to adapt to different situations. Those with a high level of awareness tend to be more empathetic, self-aware, and able to communicate effectively with others. Awareness is a crucial character quality that can lead to personal growth, better relationships, and increased success in various aspects of life.

Increased awareness can lead to the discovery of previously unnoticed information in various ways. Being more aware of your surroundings can help you notice subtle details or patterns previously overlooked. This heightened level of mindfulness can uncover hidden connections or relationships that may provide new insights. Awareness can also help recognize gaps in knowledge or understanding. By actively seeking out information and staying curious, you may identify areas where you lack sufficient information or where misconceptions exist. This awareness can prompt you to delve deeper into specific topics or seek out expertise from others to fill those gaps.

Awareness of new developments or advancements in a particular field can inspire you to explore uncharted territory and discover novel information. Staying informed about current trends, research findings, or technological breakthroughs can open up opportunities for learning and expanding your knowledge base. Cultivating awareness through mindfulness, curiosity, and staying updated can significantly enhance the chances of discovering new and valuable information previously unidentified or overlooked. Improving these skills involves being present and attentive in various aspects of life.

Ways to improve awareness skills:

1. *Mindfulness practice:* Engage in activities like meditation, praying, or deep breathing exercises to focus on the present moment.

2. *Observation exercises:* Pay close attention to your surroundings, noticing details you may have overlooked before. Be intentional and choose to be aware and perceptive.

3. *Reflective journaling:* Write down your thoughts, emotions, and observations regularly to better understand yourself and your environment. Review what is written frequently and monitor the progression of your thoughts.

4. *Active listening:* Practice listening without judgment and fully engaging with the speaker to grasp their perspective.

5. *Mindful walking:* Take time to walk in nature or a quiet area while being fully present and aware of your surroundings.

6. *Body scan meditation:* Focus on different parts of your body to recognize any tension and promote relaxation.

7. *Regular breaks:* Take short breaks throughout the day to recenter yourself and refocus your attention. Set reminders if you need to at first until you get into a regular routine.

8. *Engage in new experiences:* Try new activities or hobbies to stimulate your senses and broaden your perspective. Make observations about them and consider how they affected you. Incorporating these practices into your daily routine can strengthen your awareness skills and cultivate a deeper connection with yourself and the world around you.

9. *Be intentional:* It takes deliberate thought to focus on more awareness of yourself and your surroundings. Practice being more intentional.

Resourcefulness is a valuable character quality that refers to the ability to find creative solutions to challenges or problems using the resources at hand. Resourceful people are able to think outside the box, adapt to new situations, and make the most of the resources available to them. This quality involves being proactive, innovative, and flexible in identifying and utilizing various resources effectively. Resourcefulness also entails being able to see opportunities where others might only see obstacles, making the best of any situation, and being resilient in the face of adversity. Resourcefulness is a key component of problem-solving skills and can help you navigate obstacles and achieve your goals more effectively. It is a quality that can be cultivated and developed through practice, experience, and a positive mindset.

Resourcefulness can be invaluable in a situation like this case study by enabling you to fill in any gaps or uncertainties in the instructions. By being aware of the potential for Missing Variables, despite having instructions, orders, or even a recipe, it is helpful to learn to become more resourceful.

You can start by honing problem-solving skills and fostering a growth mindset to become more resourceful. Embrace challenges as opportunities to learn and grow. Cultivate a curious attitude and seek out new knowledge and skills. Practice thinking creatively and outside the box to find solutions. Learn to adapt and be flexible in different situations.

Networking with others can also help you access a wider range of resources and perspectives. Build relationships with people who have diverse expertise and experiences. Collaborate on projects and share resources to leverage collective knowledge.

Prioritize efficiency by organizing tasks, setting goals, and managing time effectively. Develop a system for keeping track of resources and information. Stay organized and eliminate clutter to reduce distractions and optimize productivity. Embrace technology and tools that can streamline processes and enhance productivity. Stay up-to-date on the latest innovations and explore how they can benefit your endeavors. Continuously evaluate and adjust your strategies based on feedback and outcomes. Learn from failures and setbacks to improve your resourcefulness over time.

Resourcefulness is a mindset that can be developed and strengthened with practice and persistence. By being resourceful, you can more effectively navigate potentially incomplete instructions, adapt to unexpected challenges, and ultimately achieve the desired outcome.

Ways to use resourcefulness:

1. *Research*: Use available resources like the internet or other materials to gather additional information that may clarify unclear instructions.

2. *Problem-solve*: Break down the task into smaller steps and analyze what is missing or unclear. Think creatively to come up with possible solutions.

3. *Seek clarification*: Contact the person who provided the instructions to ask questions and clarify any ambiguous points.

4. *Leverage experience*: Draw from past experiences or knowledge to infer missing details and make educated guesses.

5. *Collaborate*: Engage with others who have more information or experience with the task to gain insights and guidance.

The best laid-out plans may not always come to fruition, even with the most complete instructions. Sometimes, you must draw on other skills and character qualities for a successful outcome. Intuition plays a role in project completion by allowing you to trust your instincts and make quick decisions based on past experiences and knowledge. Critical thinking helps you analyze information, identify biases, and make logical conclusions, ensuring your decisions are well-founded. Awareness is crucial in recognizing potential pitfalls, understanding the project's context, and adapting to changing circumstances. Resourcefulness enables you to find creative solutions, leverage available resources effectively, and overcome challenges efficiently.

Combining these qualities allows you to navigate complexities, gather diverse perspectives, and access a fuller range of information to inform your project completion process. Ultimately, intuition, critical thinking, awareness, and resourcefulness, along with creativity, work together to guide you toward making informed, strategic decisions that lead to successful project outcomes.

Mastering a single skill is often not enough to ensure success. Just like a symphony orchestra requires a variety of instruments to create a harmonious melody, successful instruction completion in any endeavor often demands a combination of different skills working together in perfect harmony, such as intuition, critical thinking, and resourcefulness. Consider a chef creating a gourmet meal—exceptional cooking skills alone are not enough. The chef also needs creativity, attention to detail, time management, and the ability to work well under pressure to deliver a truly extraordinary dining experience. To achieve a successful outcome, it is crucial to recognize the interconnectedness of various skills and how they complement each other. Like puzzle pieces fitting together, each skill contributes to the overall picture of success. It is the amalgamation of these diverse skills that elevates an individual or a team toward their goals. So, remember to hone not just one skill but a diverse set of skills that can work hand in hand to lead you to a successful instructional outcome. Embrace the beauty of versatility and watch as your efforts blossom into remarkable achievements.

 Reflect:

1. Recall a situation where you followed instructions meticulously yet had an unfavorable outcome. Describe how this affected you. Describe how you felt. How did you respond? Journal your answers.

2. What have you learned about the effectiveness of complete instructions as a result of this chapter? What have you learned about having *incomplete* instructions? How does this compare to your thoughts in the past? Journal your answers.

3. What part of the suggested resolutions do you find most challenging? How will you choose to respond in the future to a project completed using instructions that turned out unfavorably? What can you do to ensure a better outcome? Journal your answers.

4. What are some dangers of not being prepared for unexpected outcomes regarding instructions? What are some of the

benefits of intuition and critical thinking? Journal regarding the plans you will implement to improve these skills.

5. What are some benefits of awareness and resourcefulness? How can you improve these skills? Who is your accountability partner for venting in unexpected conditions where you followed guidelines meticulously? Journal the reasons you value this person.

6. Find ways to program intuition, resourcefulness, awareness, and critical thinking into your "preprogram." More information about how to "Reprogram Your Pre-Program" is found in *Elevate Your Mind to Success, Success Is Ele-MENTAL*, and at www.DrJillFandrich.com.

7. How will you utilize these skills to help other people? Journal your answers.

8. Who will you share this information with? Who will benefit most from it? Journal your answers.

9. Apply critical thinking to the information you learned. More about critical thinking is found in *Who Connects Your Dots?, Medically Speaking, Who Connects Your Dots?*, and *Students: Who Connects Your Dots?*

10. Practice the skills you learned daily. Journal and monitor your progress.

CHAPTER 10

CASE STUDY NINE: TESTY TEENAGERS

In a small town, Kyle, a rebellious teenager, fiercely resisted his mother's attempts to guide him. Kyle's unpredictable behavior constantly kept his mother on edge as she struggled to understand her son's defiance. Kyle's wild nature led him to skip school, stay out late, and hang out with a risky group of friends. No matter how hard his mother tried to set boundaries and enforce rules, Kyle always found a way to break free and push against any form of control. One night, Kyle's mother received a call from the police, informing her that Kyle had been caught shoplifting. Devastated and heartbroken, his mother realized that her attempts to control Kyle had only pushed him further away.

Free will, a mind of their own, and the influence of others are the Missing Variables for teenagers and other people in general. As children begin to lose their dependency and realize they are capable of making their own decisions, they branch off from their parents and guardians, seeking to become independent and self-sufficient, whether or not it is in their best interests.

There are many phases a teenager goes through and many reasons why they pull away and become someone you no longer recognize. Teenagers may stop listening and become rebellious due to various factors such as seeking independence, testing boundaries, asserting their individuality, or feeling misunderstood. During adolescence, they undergo significant physical, emotional, and cognitive changes, which can lead to heightened emotions and a desire to challenge authority figures. Peer influence, social pressures, and hormonal changes can also contribute to their rebellious behavior. It is essential for parents and caregivers to understand that this phase is a normal part of development, communicate openly, set clear expectations, and show empathy toward the teenager's feelings. Building a trusting and supportive relationship can help navigate this challenging period and foster healthy communication between parents and teenagers.

Challenging authority is a common concern for parents or guardians of teenagers. They may seek to challenge authority for various reasons, including the desire for independence, the need to assert their individuality, and the natural urge to test boundaries. During adolescence, individuals undergo significant cognitive, emotional, and social development, leading to a greater sense of autonomy and self-awareness. This can sometimes result in questioning established rules and norms as teenagers strive to establish their own identities and beliefs.

Teenagers often have a heightened sensitivity to perceived injustices or inconsistencies in authority figures, leading them to challenge and question decisions or rules that they see as unfair or unreasonable. The desire for peer acceptance and the influence of social dynamics can also play a role in teenagers challenging authority, as they may be seeking to gain status or recognition within their peer group. Challenging authority figures can be a natural part of adolescent development as teenagers navigate the complexities of growing up and forming their own values and beliefs. It is important for people in authority to engage in open and respectful communication with teenagers while also setting clear boundaries and expectations to promote healthy and constructive interactions.

Kip had always followed the rules set by his parents and teachers. But as he entered his rebellious phase, he began testing authority due to his newfound sense of free will. Kip started staying out past curfew, skipping classes, and arguing with his parents about their strict rules. His actions caused tension at home and school, as he challenged the authority figures in his life at every turn. Kip felt a rush of independence and power as he pushed back against the constraints placed upon him. However, his defiance led to consequences he had not anticipated—his grades plummeted, he lost his parents' trust, and he became isolated from his friends.

During adolescence, teens undergo numerous physical, emotional, and cognitive changes that can be challenging to navigate. It is helpful if these changes are recognized so they can be better understood.

Understanding these changes can help parents, educators, and caregivers better support teens through this transformative stage of development.

Changes teens encounter:

1. *Physical changes:* Teens experience rapid physical growth, changes in body shape, and the onset of puberty, which can lead to heightened self-consciousness and body image issues.

2. *Hormonal fluctuations:* Hormones play a crucial role in the development of teenagers, influencing their physical growth, emotions, and behavior. Fluctuations in hormone levels during adolescence can lead to mood swings, increased stress, and changes in energy levels. These hormonal changes can also impact sleep patterns, appetite, and cognitive function. Hormones significantly affect how teenagers transition from childhood to adulthood, shaping their identity and influencing their relationships with others. By understanding and managing these hormonal changes, teens can better cope with the challenges of adolescence and enhance their overall well-being.

3. *Brain development:* The adolescent brain undergoes significant development, particularly in areas related to impulse control, decision-making, and emotional regulation. This can lead to risk-taking behaviors and struggles with self-control. The teenage brain is a complex and fascinating work in progress, still in the process of maturing. Scientific research indicates that the brain continues to develop well into a person's twenties, with crucial areas responsible for decision-making, impulse control, and emotional regulation still undergoing significant changes during adolescence. This ongoing development explains why teenagers often exhibit behaviors that can seem impulsive or irrational. The prefrontal cortex, the brain region responsible for planning, reasoning, and decision-making, is one of the last areas to fully mature. This process generally continues until a person reaches their mid-twenties when the brain fully

develops. Understanding this gradual development helps shed light on why teenagers may struggle with certain aspects of decision-making and emotional control. The teenage brain is a dynamic and evolving system that requires time to reach its full potential. As people progress through their twenties, they can expect to experience improved cognitive abilities, better emotional regulation, and more mature decision-making skills as the brain continues to mature and refine its neural connections.

4. *Identity formation*: Teens are exploring their sense of self, values, beliefs, and aspirations, which can result in identity confusion and the need for autonomy. In a world where insecurity runs rampant, some adults are passing on their doubts and fears to impressionable teens, leading to confusion about their own identities. These adults, grappling with their own insecurities, may project their uncertainties onto younger generations, fostering self-doubt and internal conflict in teens. As a result, the vulnerable minds of teenagers can become clouded with uncertainty, making it difficult for them to understand and accept their God-given identity. It is crucial to recognize this cycle of insecurity and actively work to break it by promoting self-awareness, confidence, and authenticity in both adults and teens. By addressing these underlying issues and encouraging open dialogue, you can help young individuals navigate their identities with clarity and confidence, empowering them to embrace who God made them to be.

5. *Social pressures*: Peer influence, social media, and societal expectations can all contribute to increased stress, anxiety, and pressure to fit in. Social pressure can significantly impact teenagers as they navigate through the complexities of adolescence. Teenagers often feel pressured to conform to certain standards or behaviors, whether it be the influence of peers, societal expectations, or media portrayal of idealized lifestyles. This pressure can manifest in various ways, such as changing their appearance, adopting specific interests, or

making decisions based on the fear of judgment or rejection. The desire to fit in and be accepted can lead to teenagers compromising their values, engaging in risky behaviors, or feeling immense stress and anxiety. Understanding the power of social pressure on teenagers is crucial in promoting their mental well-being and encouraging them to develop a strong sense of self-confidence and resilience. By fostering open communication, providing guidance, and promoting a positive self-image, you can help teenagers navigate social pressures more effectively and empower them to make choices that align with their values and aspirations.

Determined to mend their fractured relationship, Kyle's mother decided to take a different approach. Instead of trying to control him, she chose to listen, understand, and support her son. Through open communication and unconditional love, Kyle slowly began to let his guard down and reveal the underlying struggles that fueled his rebellious behavior. As their bond grew stronger, Kyle gradually learned to trust his mother and accept her guidance. Together, they navigated the challenges of adolescence, finding a balance between freedom and responsibility. Through patience and understanding, they discovered that love and connection were more powerful than any form of control.

Listening to teenagers can significantly impact their growth and behavior in several ways. Listening intently helps to build trust and strengthen the parent-child or mentor-mentee relationship, fostering open communication and understanding. By actively listening to teenagers, adults can gain insight into their thoughts, feelings, and perspectives, which can help identify any issues or challenges they may face. It validates their feelings and experiences, making them feel understood, respected, and valued. This can boost their self-esteem and confidence, leading to improved emotional well-being and mental health. By listening attentively, adults can also provide much-needed support and guidance, helping teenagers navigate through difficult situations and make informed decisions.

As Kip continued down an isolated path, he soon realized that true freedom came not from rebellion but from making responsible choices. Through a series of experiences and lessons, he learned to balance his newfound free will with respect for authority. In the end, Kip discovered that testing authority was not about defiance but about finding his own voice and identity within the boundaries set by his parents.

Listening to teenagers encourages them to express themselves constructively, develop their communication skills, and learn to articulate their needs and opinions effectively. This can enhance their self-awareness and emotional intelligence, leading to more mature and responsible behavior. Listening can promote positive growth and development by fostering healthy relationships, improving mental well-being, and empowering them to make positive choices in various aspects of their lives.

Bella always had a strong sense of independence and free will. She often clashed with her mother, Emily, who tried to instill values of respect and responsibility in her daughter. One day, after a heated argument about Bella's curfew, she let her mouth run wild and said hurtful things to her mother. Emily was hurt and disappointed by Bella's words, but she understood that her daughter was just asserting her independence and testing her boundaries.

Openly communicating with teens can significantly improve your relationship with them in several ways. It builds trust and mutual respect between you and the teenager, creating a more positive and supportive relationship. Listening actively and showing genuine interest in what they say demonstrate that you value their thoughts and feelings. Open communication allows for a better understanding of the teen's perspective, which can lead to more effective problem-solving and conflict resolution. You can address issues before they escalate and work together to find mutually beneficial solutions by engaging in open discussions.

Instead of reacting in anger, Emily decided to have a calm and honest conversation with Bella about the importance of respect and communication in their relationship. Bella realized that her words had caused pain to her mother, and she apologized sincerely. Through this experience, both mother and daughter learned valuable lessons about the power of words and the importance of empathy and understanding. From that day on, Bella made a conscious effort to think before speaking and to communicate her feelings more positively and respectfully.

Their relationship grew stronger as they navigated the challenges of adolescence together, guided by love, patience, and mutual respect.

Open communication fosters a sense of connection and intimacy between you and the teen, strengthening the bond and promoting a sense of belonging. This can lead to increased feelings of security and support for the teenager, which is crucial during their formative years. By establishing open communication with teens, you create a safe and welcoming environment where they feel comfortable expressing themselves and sharing their thoughts and emotions. This can lead to a more positive and fulfilling relationship built on trust, understanding, and empathy.

Creating a safe environment for teenagers can greatly contribute to building their confidence. One way is by providing consistent support and encouragement from parents, teachers, and peers. When teenagers feel accepted and valued, they are more likely to believe in themselves and their abilities. Setting clear boundaries and expectations can also help teenagers feel secure and confident. Knowing what is expected of them and understanding the consequences of their actions can provide a sense of structure and stability.

Offering opportunities for teenagers to take on challenges and succeed can boost their self-esteem and confidence. When teenagers are able to overcome obstacles and achieve their goals, they gain a sense of accomplishment and belief in their abilities. Promoting open communication and providing a safe space for teenagers to express their thoughts and feelings can help them feel heard and understood. This can lead to increased self-awareness and confidence in their own identities. A safe environment that fosters support, clear boundaries, opportunities for growth, and open communication can help teenagers develop the confidence they need to navigate the challenges of adolescence and beyond.

It Is difficult to watch children leave one phase of life and enter the next, especially as they enter the teenage phase! It may be the first phase of their lives that required letting go of some of the control you had in raising, protecting, and guiding them. When dealing with a teenager, a parent can relinquish control by practicing open communication, setting boundaries, and allowing the teenager to make decisions and learn from their mistakes. It is essential for the parent to listen to their teenager's perspective, validate their feelings, and encourage independence and responsibility. By providing guidance and support rather than control, the parent can empower teenagers to make their own choices and develop important life skills.

It may also be helpful for the parent to acknowledge that their teenager is growing and changing and that a shift in the parent-child dynamic is natural during this phase of development. It is important to trust in the values and lessons that have been instilled in teenagers and to allow them the space to navigate their own path while still providing a safety net when needed. Relinquishing control does not mean abandoning the teenager or the parenting role. It means fostering a relationship built on trust, respect, and mutual understanding, which can lead to a healthier and more positive dynamic between the parent and teenager.

As a parent or guardian, it's essential to understand that you cannot fully control a teenager's free will. This is a Missing Variable that is out of your control. Adolescents are at a stage where they are developing their independence and making their own decisions. However, you can still play a crucial role in guiding and supporting them through this journey. By establishing open communication, setting boundaries, and offering advice based on your experience, you can help steer them in the right direction. Building a trusting and respectful relationship with your teenager will make them more likely to turn to you for guidance when faced with tough decisions. Remember, while you may not have control over their choices, your presence and guidance can significantly impact their development and decision-making process. Be patient, understanding, and supportive as they navigate the complexities of adolescence, and be there to provide a steady hand when they need it most.

> As the sun sets on childhood, a new dawn emerges for teenagers, embarking on a journey of self-discovery and independence. The time has come for parents to loosen the reins, allowing their fledglings to soar into the unknown. Mistakes will be made, lessons will be learned, but growth will be inevitable. In the dance of life, parents must learn to lead with a light touch, offering guidance from the sidelines as their teenagers navigate the twists and turns of adolescence. Like a safety net beneath a

high-flying trapeze artist, parents must be there to catch their teenagers when they fall while also granting them the freedom to brush themselves off and try again. This delicate balance of letting go and holding on is the ultimate test of parenthood. It requires patience, trust, and a willingness to embrace the uncertainty of the future. For teenagers, this phase represents a rite of passage, a time to spread their wings and test their limits. For parents, it is a time to step back, take a deep breath, and marvel at the beautiful chaos of watching their children grow into the unique individuals they were always meant to be.

—Jill Fandrich

 Reflect:

1. Describe a situation with a teenager that was out of your control. How did this affect you? How did you feel? How did you respond? Journal your answers.

2. What have you learned about what you *cannot* control with a teenager as a result of this chapter? What have you learned about what you *can* control? How does this compare to your thoughts in the past? Journal your answers.

3. What part of the suggested resolutions for responding to teenagers do you find most challenging? How will you choose to respond in the future to a strong-willed teenager? What can you do to ensure a better outcome? Journal your answers.

4. What are some dangers of not being prepared for an unruly teenager? What are some of the benefits of actively listening and open communication? Journal regarding the plans you will implement to improve these skills.

5. What are some benefits of understanding the changes they are undergoing? How can you improve your knowledge of this?

Who is your accountability partner for venting when you are frustrated and need to talk regarding a teenager? Journal the reasons you value this person.

6. Find ways to program active listening, effective communication, and supportiveness into your "preprogram." More information about how to "Reprogram Your Pre-Program" is found in *Elevate Your Mind to Success*, *Success Is Ele-MENTAL*, and at www.DrJillFandrich.com.

7. How will you utilize these skills to help other people? Journal your answers.

8. Who will you share this information with? Who will benefit most from it? Journal your answers.

9. Apply critical thinking to the information you learned. More about critical thinking is found in *Who Connects Your Dots?*, *Medically Speaking, Who Connects Your Dots?*, and *Students: Who Connects Your Dots?*

10. Practice the skills you learned daily. Journal and monitor your progress.

CHAPTER 11

CASE STUDY TEN: SINGLE PARENTS

Alicia's heart shattered into a million pieces as she watched her son, Noah, walk away with his father for their court-ordered shared visitation. The tears streamed down her face as she forced a smile, trying to be strong for Noah. She couldn't bear the thought of being away from him, knowing he would be under the care of his narcissistic father. As the days turned into a week, Alicia felt like a piece of her was missing. She missed Noah's laughter, his hugs, his innocent questions. But every time she dropped him off for visitation, she could see the manipulation and control her ex-husband exerted over their son. Noah's once bright eyes now held a hint of fear and confusion. Alicia fought back the urge to confront her ex-husband, knowing it would only make things worse for Noah. She clung to the hope that one day, he would see the truth and choose to protect their son. Until then, she held onto the precious moments with Noah, cherishing every second they had together, praying they would be together for good one day.

In this heartbreaking story, a single parent faces the difficult reality of parting with her child for shared visitations with a narcissistic father. The mother struggles with the emotional turmoil of entrusting her precious child to someone who prioritizes his own needs above all else. Despite her deep love and care for her child, she must navigate the painful process of co-parenting with a father who lacks empathy and understanding.

The single parent grapples with feelings of helplessness and fear for her child's well-being during these visitations, knowing that the father's self-centered nature may impact the child's emotional development and sense of security. She must find strength within herself to advocate for her child's best interests while also trying to maintain a sense of stability and normalcy in their lives. Through this challenging experience, the single parent demonstrates unwavering resilience and determination to protect her child from the negative effects of the father's behavior. Her unconditional love and sacrifice shine through as she navigates the complex dynamics of co-parenting with grace and courage, all for the sake of her beloved child's well-being.

Have you ever been in a situation as described in this case study? This is about as heartbreaking as it can get. Yet, the event is beyond your control as the court not only demands but encourages the visitation. The Missing Variable is a court-order visitation and the other parent's actions you cannot control.

Single parents may experience a range of intense emotions during this challenging situation. You may feel profound sadness and heartache at being separated from your child, as well as anxiety about how the narcissistic parent will treat the child. You may also feel a sense of powerlessness and frustration at not being able to protect your child from potential harm or emotional manipulation.

You may experience guilt for exposing your child to difficult situations and questioning your decisions around co-parenting. You may feel anger and resentment toward the narcissistic parent for causing distress to both you and your child. You may also struggle with feelings of isolation and loneliness during the times when your child is not with you. Overall, you may grapple with a complex mix of emotions, including sadness, anxiety, powerlessness, guilt, anger, resentment, and loneliness, while navigating shared visitations with a narcissistic parent. It is essential for you to prioritize self-care and seek support from friends, family, or a therapist to help you process and cope with these challenging emotions.

As a single parent, coping while your child is away on visitation with a narcissistic parent or even a good parent in general can be challenging. It's important to prioritize your own well-being and that of your child.

Here are some tips to help you cope:

1. *Self-care*: Use this time to focus on yourself. Engaging in activities you enjoy or find relaxing, such as reading, practicing mindfulness, or meditation, could help calm your mind and

reduce stress. Take care of your physical and emotional well-being and prioritize self-care. Take time for yourself by reading a book, walking, going to the spa, or watching a movie. Exercise releases endorphins and boosts your mood. Pamper yourself with a relaxing detox bath, skincare routine, or a favorite hobby. Prepare nutritious meals for yourself to nourish your body and mind. Get enough rest and prioritize sleep to recharge your energy levels. Engage in creative outlets like painting, writing, puzzling, or crafting to express yourself. Practice gratitude by focusing on the positive aspects of your life and experiences. Taking care of yourself is essential to recharge and better support your child when he returns.

2. *Staying connected*: Keep in touch with your child through phone calls, video chats, or messages. This can help you feel connected and reassure you that they are doing well.

3. *Social support*: Reach out to friends, family, or support groups for emotional support and companionship during this time. During a child's visitation, you may experience feelings of loneliness, anxiety, and worry. Leaning on loved ones or support groups can provide essential support to cope with these emotions. Family and friends can offer emotional comfort, understanding, and reassurance during this challenging time. They can help alleviate your feelings of isolation by providing companionship and a listening ear. Loved ones can assist with practical tasks such as running errands, completing household chores, or simply spending time together to distract you from negative thoughts. By sharing your concerns and seeking guidance from those close to you, you can find solace in knowing you are not alone in your struggles. Maintaining open communication with loved ones can strengthen relationships and create a sense of unity and solidarity. Connecting with a support system can also help you build resilience and develop coping strategies for managing your emotions effectively. Ultimately, leaning on loved ones during a child's visitation can offer a source of

comfort, encouragement, and strength to help you navigate this challenging period.

4. *Vent or grieve privately*: Allowing yourself time to vent or grieve by yourself while your child is away at shared visitation can have several benefits. It provides you with a safe space to express your emotions without worrying about how it may affect your child. Venting or grieving alone can help you process your feelings more effectively and come to terms with your emotions in a healthy way. It can also prevent you from unintentionally burdening your child with your emotions, allowing them to enjoy their time with the other parent without feeling responsible for your well-being. Additionally, taking time for yourself can help you recharge and regain emotional balance, which can ultimately benefit your relationship with your child when he returns. By allowing yourself this time to prioritize your own emotional needs, you are better equipped to be present and supportive of your child when they are with you. So, cry, scream, yell, or pound on the floor. Take this time to drain your heightened emotions so you can move forward healthily.

5. *Productivity*: Use the time to catch up on work, tasks, hobbies, or projects you may not have time for when your child is with you. This will help distract you and pass the time until you are reunited with your child. Being productive can help you cope during your child's visitation by allowing you to focus your energy and attention on positive activities. It can provide a sense of purpose, accomplishment, and fulfillment during what may otherwise be a challenging time. By staying busy and productive, you can maintain a sense of routine and structure in your day, which can be comforting during your child's absence. Productivity can also distract you from negative thoughts or worries, helping you stay mentally and emotionally healthy. Setting goals and completing tasks can boost self-esteem and confidence, reinforcing your ability to handle difficult situations. Being productive during a child's visitation can be a way for you to take care of yourself and maintain a positive outlook,

ultimately benefiting both your well-being and your relationship with your child. The opportunity may even motivate you to turn something sour into a business success. Turn the negativity into a positive determination to improve your current situation.

6. *Planning ahead*: Have a plan in place for how you will spend your time while your child is away. This can help alleviate feelings of loneliness or boredom. Remember, it is okay to feel a range of emotions during this time, but by taking care of yourself and staying connected, you can cope more effectively until your child returns. Think of places you haven't been able to visit for a while. Maybe there is a play or musical that would bore your child to tears, but you would enjoy it. Or, start a new TV or movie series you have been meaning to watch as something to look forward to and indulge in. It's beneficial to both you and your child to find things you enjoy today and nurture your own well-being. Take this time for things you like to do.

7. *Seeking therapy*: Consider seeking therapy or counseling to process your feelings and emotions during this difficult time. This can benefit you in coping with the emotions that arise when your child is away at visitation. Through therapy, you can explore and process your feelings of loneliness, separation anxiety, and guilt. A therapist can provide a safe space to express your concerns and fears, helping you develop coping strategies and improving your emotional well-being. Therapy can assist you in managing stress, building resilience, and enhancing communication skills that can strengthen the parent-child relationship. By working with a therapist, you can develop effective ways to support your child during visitation periods and navigate the challenges of co-parenting. Therapy can also help you better understand your needs and boundaries, empowering you to prioritize self-care and balance your personal life and parenting responsibilities. Overall, therapy offers valuable support and guidance to single parents facing the unique challenges of raising a child while managing visitation arrangements.

8. *Well-being*: Focus on improving your well-being and personal growth while apart from your child. Focusing on this as a single parent during your child's visitation can greatly help you cope with the situation. By taking care of yourself physically, emotionally, and mentally, you can better manage feelings of loneliness, anxiety, or stress that may arise during this time. Engaging in self-care activities such as building immunity, exercising, healthy eating, developing a positive mindset, finding new ways to relax, practicing mindfulness, connecting with friends or support groups, or pursuing hobbies can help you stay grounded and positive. Prioritizing your well-being allows you to recharge and maintain a healthy mindset, which in turn benefits your relationship with your child. By nurturing yourself, you are better equipped to be present and attentive when your child returns from visitation, fostering a strong and supportive environment for them. Remember that taking care of yourself is not selfish but essential for your overall well-being and ability to be the best parent you can be.

9. *Writing activities*: Write letters or keep a journal to express your thoughts and feelings, even if you cannot communicate directly with your child. Writing letters or journaling can be a beneficial coping mechanism for you while your child is at visitation. It provides a private outlet to express emotions, fears, and hopes. This process can help you release pent-up feelings and clarify your thoughts. Through writing, you can reflect on your experiences and identify coping strategies for dealing with the separation. Writing letters to your child during visitation can serve as a way to maintain a connection and express love and support. It allows you to share your feelings, memories, and encouragement, which can strengthen the bond between you and the child. Receiving letters back from the child can also provide comfort and reassurance during the separation. Journaling can help you track your emotional journey, document your experiences, and monitor your mental well-being. It enables self-reflection and growth, as well as serves as a tool for processing difficult emotions and finding solace in

writing. You can keep track of what your most effective coping mechanism is and monitor your progress. Overall, writing letters or journaling can be a therapeutic practice for you to navigate the challenges of visitation periods and cope with the temporary separation from your child.

10. *Assurance*: Remind yourself that the visitation is temporary and that you will be reunited with your child soon. Feeling a range of emotions during this time is okay, and seeking support from others can help you navigate this challenging situation.

11. *Leaning on your relationship with God*: Prayer and time in the Bible can provide comfort, strength, and guidance while your child is away on visitation. Through prayer, you can express your fears, worries, and hopes to God, finding peace in the belief that you are not alone in your struggles. By reading and reflecting on the Bible, you can find stories and verses that offer solace, encouragement, and wisdom to help you navigate this difficult time. Drawing upon the teachings of the Bible can remind you of the importance of faith, patience, and trust in God's plan, even when faced with challenges and uncertainty. It can also serve as a source of hope, comfort, and reassurance that your child is in God's hands and that you can find strength in your faith to cope with his absence. Prayer and studying the Bible can help you maintain a sense of connection to your child spiritually, even when physically apart. It can provide a sense of comfort and resilience as you navigate this period of separation.

Resilience is a character quality vital for coping while your child is away. It can greatly benefit you during this time by providing you with the strength and coping mechanisms needed to navigate separation challenges. By fostering resilience, you can effectively cope with the temporary separation from your child and emerge stronger from the experience.

Ways resilience can help with a temporary separation from your child:

1. *Positive mindset*: Resilience helps you to maintain a positive outlook despite the separation, focusing on the idea that this time apart is temporary and will help strengthen your bond with your child.

2. *Adaptability*: Resilience enables you to adapt to changes in routines and schedules during visitation periods, allowing you to find new ways to stay productive and take care of yourself.

3. *Social support*: Resilience encourages you to seek support from friends, family, or support groups, providing you with a strong network to lean on during this challenging time.

4. *Self-care*: Resilience emphasizes the importance of self-care activities such as exercise, hobbies, or relaxation techniques to help you recharge and stay emotionally healthy while your child is away.

5. *Problem-solving skills*: Resilience equips you with problem-solving skills to handle any unexpected issues or emotions that may arise during the visitation period.

Resilience is the ability to bounce back from challenges, setbacks, and adversity. There are tips you can consider to enhance your resilience. By incorporating these strategies into your daily life, you can cultivate greater resilience and journey through life's challenges with strength and grace.

Ways to improve your resilience:

1. *Cultivate a positive mindset*: Focus on solutions rather than problems and practice gratitude and optimism.

2. *Build a strong support system*: Surround yourself with positive, supportive people who can provide encouragement and help you navigate tough times.

3. *Develop coping strategies*: Learn healthy ways to manage stress, such as exercise, meditation, deep breathing, or engaging in hobbies.

4. *Embrace change*: Accept that change is a natural part of life and practice adapting to new situations with flexibility and openness.

5. *Set realistic goals*: Break down larger goals into smaller, achievable steps to maintain motivation and build confidence.

6. *Maintain a healthy lifestyle*: Prioritize proper nutrition, regular exercise, and sufficient sleep to bolster your physical and mental well-being.

7. *Learn from setbacks*: View failures or challenges as opportunities for growth and self-improvement, and use them as lessons to enhance your resilience in the future.

Feeling powerless while your child is away on visitation with the other parent is a common challenge for many parents. It can be addressed similarly to the previous coping mechanisms in this chapter. It's important to acknowledge and accept these feelings, as they are natural and valid. To cope with this feeling, focus on maintaining open and honest communication with your child during his time away. Stay connected through phone calls, video chats, or letters to reassure yourself and your child of the love and bond you share. Engage in self-care activities to help manage your emotions, such as exercise, meditation, or spending time with supportive friends and family. Keep yourself busy with hobbies or tasks that bring you joy and fulfillment. Remember that your child's well-being is a priority; trusting the other parent to care for him can alleviate some of your worries. Seek support from a therapist or counselor who can provide guidance and strategies for coping with feelings of powerlessness. It's okay to feel vulnerable and seek help when needed. By caring for yourself and staying connected with your child, you can navigate these challenging emotions and strengthen your relationship with your child.

Maintaining a positive mindset during visitation with the other parent can help you navigate this challenging time with grace and resilience. By focusing on positivity, you can alleviate anxiety and stress, allowing you to make the most of your time apart from your child. Embracing a positive outlook can help you stay calm, grounded, and emotionally stable, ensuring you can support your child's well-being even when you are not together. Trusting in the bond you share with your child and believing that this time apart can strengthen your relationship in different ways is essential. By maintaining a positive mindset, you can cherish the moments you have with your child, no matter the distance, and look forward to reuniting with a heart full of love and joy. Remember, staying positive not only benefits you but also sets a healthy example for your child on how to navigate challenges with resilience and optimism.

Developing a positive mindset while your child is away on visitation can be tricky. Yet, it is beneficial for both you and your child. It is normal to feel a range of emotions when your child is away, but focusing on building a positive mindset is a healthy choice.

Ways to help you maintain a positive outlook while your child is away:

1. *Quality time*: Focus on the quality time you will have with your child when they return.

2. *Practice gratitude*: Take time daily to reflect on things you are grateful for, no matter how small they may seem.

3. *Surround yourself with positive influences*: Spend time with people who uplift and support you.

4. *Challenge negative thoughts*: Identify and replace negative thought patterns with more positive and realistic ones.

5. *Set goals*: Having clear goals and working toward them can boost your confidence and motivation. It's okay to set them in small segments during this challenging time. You deserve an easy win.

6. *Practice self-care*: Take care of your physical, emotional, and mental well-being, as it can impact your mindset.

7. *Focus on the present moment*: Practice mindfulness and stay present instead of dwelling on the past or worrying about the future.

8. *Learn from setbacks*: Instead of seeing failures as obstacles, view them as opportunities for growth and learning.

9. *Engage in activities that bring you joy*: Pursue hobbies and activities that make you happy and help you relax.

10. *Listen to positive audiobooks or podcasts*: Take time to listen to audiobooks or podcasts that elevate your mind. Or select uplifting music or meditations that help declutter your mind and set it in a positive direction.

11. *Practice positive affirmations*: Repeat affirmations that reinforce positive beliefs about yourself and your God-given abilities.

12. *Seek professional help if needed*: If you are struggling to develop a positive mindset, consider seeking the help of a therapist or counselor.

When faced with a situation involving shared visitation of a child that is beyond your control, it's important to acknowledge your limitations and focus on what you can influence. While you may not be able to dictate the schedule or circumstances of the shared visitation, you can control how you respond to it. Embracing self-care practices such as mindfulness, hobbies, exercise, filling yourself with positive influences, or socializing can help you cope with the situation in a healthy manner. It's vital to communicate openly with the other party involved and establish boundaries that prioritize your well-being and that of your child. It's okay to seek support from friends, family, or a therapist to navigate through this challenging time. By reframing your perspective and finding ways to enjoy your alone time, you can cultivate a sense of balance and resilience that will benefit both you and your child in the long run.

In the delicate dance of shared visitation, your single-parent heart beats with uncertainty and resilience. Juggling the weight of responsibilities while navigating the ebb and flow of emotions, each visit becomes a bittersweet reminder of what once was and what could have been. The echoes of laughter and tears linger in the air, painting a complex tapestry of love and longing. As the clock ticks mercilessly, you grapple with the ever-present fear of missing out on precious moments, all the while trying to foster a sense of normalcy for your child. Bound by duty and commitment, you strive to shield your little one from the storm brewing within, carrying the weight of unspoken sacrifices with grace and fortitude. Through tear-stained smiles and whispered prayers, you can find solace in the fleeting moments of connection and understanding. Each shared visit becomes a testament to your unwavering strength and unwavering love, a silent homage to the challenges faced and conquered with unwavering determination.

Reflect:

1. Describe an experience you encountered involving single parenting. Describe how this affected you. Describe how you felt. How did you respond? Journal your answers.

2. What have you learned about what you *cannot* control in a shared visitation scenario as a result of this chapter? What have you learned about what you *can* control in a shared visitation scenario? How does this compare to your thoughts in the past? Journal your answers.

3. What part of the suggested resolutions do you find most challenging? How will you choose to respond in the future if you or a loved one faces this circumstance? What can you do to ensure a better outcome? Journal your answers.

4. What are some dangers of not being prepared for a time of loneliness or powerlessness? What are some benefits of self-care and support during times of sadness? Journal regarding the plans you will implement.

5. ACTIVITY: Set aside an empty tissue box. Cut paper or index cards into approximately 2" x 2" or as desired. Write down your most painful feelings on the paper or card, using as many as necessary to vent fully. When finished, fold the paper or card in half and place it into the box, never to be seen again. Repeat as needed until the box is full, then dispose of the box *and* the negative feelings as well. Imagine the negativity dissipating entirely.

6. What are some benefits of understanding the emotions involved in time away from a child? What are the benefits of focusing on a positive and healthy mindset? How can you improve your knowledge of this? Who is your accountability partner for venting when you are sad or lonely and need to talk to someone? Journal the reasons you value this person.

7. Find ways to program resilience, a positive mindset, and coping mechanisms into your "preprogram." More information about how to "Reprogram Your Pre-Program" is found in *Elevate Your Mind to Success, Success Is Ele-MENTAL*, and at www. DrJillFandrich.com.

8. How will you utilize these skills to help other people? Journal your answers.

9. Who will you share this information with? Who will benefit most from it? Journal your answers.

10. Apply critical thinking to the information you learned. More about critical thinking is found in *Who Connects Your Dots?*, *Medically Speaking, Who Connects Your Dots?*, and *Students: Who Connects Your Dots?*

11. Practice the skills you learned daily. Journal and monitor your progress.

CHAPTER 12

CASE STUDY ELEVEN: FLUCTUATING FINANCES

Joe was a seasoned banker known for his meticulous planning and confident decision-making. One day, he received a lucrative offer to invest in a new tech startup. Convinced of his ability to assess risks, Joe plunged into the opportunity without much hesitation. Joe's confidence in controlling the situation grew as the investment progressed. He monitored the market trends, evaluated the company's performance, and reassured his colleagues that everything was going according to plan. However, as time passed, unexpected challenges emerged. The tech industry faced a sudden downturn, causing the startup's value to plummet. Joe's initial projections and risk assessments proved inadequate in the face of this unforeseen crisis. Panicked and overwhelmed, Joe realized he was not as in control as he had believed. The situation spiraled out of his hands, leading to financial losses for both the bank and himself.

Unexplained or unexpected events can throw a wrench in any plan. In this case study, Joe worked very hard and utilized his expertise in his investment decisions. Despite monitoring trends and evaluating performance, the decline of the tech industry's value proved to be the Missing Variable. Despite meticulous planning and careful calculation, financial losses ensued.

It was a humbling experience for Joe, teaching him the valuable lesson that even the most experienced professionals can be blindsided by unpredictable circumstances. Joe learned to approach future decisions with more caution and humility, recognizing that true control is an illusion in the ever-changing landscape of the financial world.

Cautiousness is a character quality and can be integrated with confident actions by being mindful of potential risks and uncertainties while still moving forward with conviction. This involves a balance between bold decision-making and prudent consideration of consequences. By applying cautiousness to confident actions, you can enhance your decision-making process, minimize potential drawbacks, and increase the likelihood of successful outcomes.

Ways to apply cautiousness to confident actions:

1. *Risk assessment:* Evaluate the potential risks and benefits before taking action. Identify potential pitfalls and have contingency plans in place.

2. *Research and preparation:* Gather relevant information and resources to make informed decisions. Thoroughly assess the situation before proceeding.

3. *Seek advice:* Consult with trusted professionals or experts to gain different perspectives and insights. Incorporate feedback into your decision-making process.

4. *Start small:* Begin with manageable steps to test your ideas and strategies before committing fully. Gradually increase your level of confidence as you gain experience and results.

5. *Reflect and adapt:* Continuously review your progress, learn from your experiences, and make necessary adjustments along the way. Stay flexible and open to change.

6. *Diversify:* Anytime finances are involved, it may be prudent to diversify resources and not "put all your eggs into one basket," so to speak.

7. *Think critically:* Critical thinking will help in making logical decisions, thereby increasing your confidence in making logical and objective choices and decisions.

8. *Expect the unexpected:* Expecting the unexpected is a valuable form of cautiousness that can be applied to confident actions. You can approach decisions with greater confidence and resilience by anticipating various possibilities and being

prepared for unforeseen outcomes. This mindset allows for adaptability in the face of uncertainty and helps mitigate potential risks or challenges that may arise. Embracing the idea of the unexpected empowers you to make informed choices while remaining open to new opportunities and unforeseen circumstances. By acknowledging and preparing for the unexpected, you can navigate confidently through uncertainties and challenges, demonstrating a proactive and strategic approach to decision-making.

When you find yourself in a situation where you believe you are in control, only to realize you are not, it can be a humbling experience. This could happen in various aspects of life, such as in relationships, careers, financial situations, or personal goals. For example, someone may have thought he had his career perfectly planned out, only to unexpectedly lose his job due to circumstances beyond his control. This realization can serve as a reminder of the unpredictable nature of life and the limitations of control over external factors. Similarly, in a relationship, you may believe you have a strong grasp on the dynamics and direction, only to have a significant disagreement or breakup that exposes your lack of control over the other person's feelings or decisions. In both scenarios, the humbling experience can lead to introspection, growth, and a deeper understanding of your vulnerability and limitations. It can also foster empathy toward others who may be facing similar challenges. Ultimately, such experiences can serve as valuable lessons in resilience, adaptability, and acceptance of the uncertainties in life.

Humility is a character quality or trait characterized by modesty, meekness, and a lack of arrogance or pride. It involves an honest and realistic assessment of your own abilities, achievements, and limitations without boasting or seeking excessive attention. Humble people are open to feedback, willing to learn from others, and show respect toward everyone regardless of their status or position. Humility is often associated with a sense of inner strength, self-awareness, and a genuine desire to serve others rather than seeking personal gain or recognition. It involves acknowledging mistakes, accepting constructive criticism, and maintaining a sense of gratitude and perspective amidst success or failure. Humility can lead to stronger relationships, improved communication, and overall personal growth and development.

To incorporate more humility into decision-making while maintaining confidence and control, it is important to acknowledge that humility does not equate to weakness or lack of confidence. You can strike a balance between humility and confidence in your decision-making process by incorporating these strategies, leading to more well-rounded and effective outcomes.

Humility strategies:

1. *Active listening:* Take the time to listen to different viewpoints and perspectives before making a decision. Recognize that you may not have all the answers, and be open to learning from others.

2. *Seek feedback:* Encourage feedback from peers, mentors, or team members to gain insights to help you make more informed decisions. Recognize that constructive criticism can lead to growth and improvement.

3. *Contemplation:* Contemplation is a humility strategy in the decision-making process by fostering a mindset of openness, reflection, and self-awareness. When you engage in contemplative practices such as meditation, introspection, or deep thinking, you are more likely to approach decisions humbly. Through contemplation, you can recognize the limitations of your own knowledge and perspectives, leading to a willingness to consider alternative viewpoints and possibilities. This helps prevent arrogance or overconfidence in decision-making and encourages a more collaborative and inclusive approach. Contemplation also allows you to connect with your values, beliefs, and emotions, enabling you to make decisions that are aligned with yourself. By reflecting deeply on a situation, you can tap into your intuition and wisdom, leading to more thoughtful and balanced decisions. In essence, incorporating contemplation into the decision-making process can cultivate humility by promoting self-awareness, openness to new ideas,

and a deeper understanding of your own motivations and biases. This can ultimately lead to more ethical, empathetic, and effective decision-making.

4. *Embrace vulnerability*: Admit when you don't have all the answers or when you make mistakes. Embracing vulnerability can build trust and foster better relationships with others.

5. *Stay open-minded*: Remain open to new ideas and be willing to adapt your decisions based on new information or feedback. Humility involves being flexible and willing to learn from your experiences.

Using cautiousness and humility in situations where control may be uncertain involves acknowledging limitations and being open to differing perspectives. Cautiousness helps in assessing risks and making informed decisions, while humility allows for a willingness to learn from others and accept feedback. In situations where control is uncertain, such as fluctuating financial trends, these traits can help navigate challenges with a balanced approach, considering both personal capabilities and external factors. By being cautious, you can avoid unnecessary risks and anticipate potential obstacles, while humility enables a readiness to adapt and collaborate with others when needed. Combining cautiousness and humility fosters a mindset of thoughtful consideration and openness to unknown variables, enhancing your ability to make sound judgments and respond effectively to changing circumstances.

Sam approached financial decisions with cautiousness and humility. He believed in taking calculated risks and avoiding impulsive choices. Despite pressure from friends to invest in get-rich-quick schemes, Sam stayed true to his principles. He diligently researched opportunities and sought advice from financial experts before making any decisions. Sam understood the importance of saving and budgeting, always living below his means to build a solid financial foundation. Through his cautious approach, Sam avoided many pitfalls that others fell into, such as scams and market crashes. While his friends boasted about their short-term gains, Sam quietly continued to grow his wealth steadily. Over time, Sam's humility allowed him to learn from his mistakes and adapt his strategies. He remained open-minded and willing to accept advice, leading to even greater success in his financial endeavors. Sam's careful and humble approach paid off. He achieved financial security and peace of mind, knowing his decisions were made thoughtfully and with a long-term perspective. Sam became an inspiration to others, showing that a combination of cautiousness and humility can lead to a better financial outcome in the end.

In the ever-changing realm of finance, uncertainty reigns supreme. Markets fluctuate, economies shift, and what was stable one moment can crumble the next. The unpredictability of the financial world can leave you feeling powerless, at the mercy of unseen forces beyond your control. But amidst this chaos lies opportunity. By understanding the nature of volatility and embracing flexibility, you can navigate these turbulent waters with grace and resilience. Instead of fearing the unknown, you can adapt your strategies, diversify your investments, and stay informed to make informed decisions in the face of uncertainty. Just as a skilled sailor adjusts his course in a storm, you, too, can learn to ride the waves of market fluctuations, leveraging your knowledge and foresight to weather the storms of economic upheaval. By staying vigilant, staying informed, embracing humility and cautiousness, and staying adaptable, you can not only survive but thrive in the unpredictable world of finance.

 Reflect:

1. Describe a financial situation where an unexpected event or trend overcame your perfect planning. Describe how this affected you. Describe how you felt. How did you respond? Journal your answers.

2. What have you learned about what you *cannot* control despite your expertise in the financial sector as a result of this chapter? What have you learned about what you *can* control? How does this compare to your thoughts in the past? Journal your answers.

3. What part of the suggested resolution of humility do you find most challenging? How will you choose to add more caution and humility in the future? What can you do to ensure a better outcome? Journal your answers.

4. What are some dangers of unpreparedness for unexpected circumstances, such as financial fluctuations? What are some benefits of expecting the unexpected? Journal regarding the plans you will implement.

5. What are some benefits of diversifying your finances? How can you improve your knowledge of this? Who is your accountability partner for venting when you are frustrated financially? Journal the reasons you value this person.

6. Find ways to program cautiousness, open-mindedness, and humility into your "preprogram." More information about how to "Reprogram Your Pre-Program" is found in *Elevate Your Mind to Success, Success Is Ele-MENTAL*, and at www. DrJillFandrich.com.

7. How will you utilize these skills to help other people? Journal your answers.

8. Who will you share this information with? Who will benefit most from it? Journal your answers.

9. Apply critical thinking to the information you learned. More about critical thinking is found in *Who Connects Your Dots?, Medically Speaking, Who Connects Your Dots?*, and *Students: Who Connects Your Dots?*

10. Practice the skills you learned daily. Journal and monitor your progress.

CHAPTER 13

Case Study Twelve: Business Blunders

Kara, a driven entrepreneur, launched her online business with detailed plans for success. She meticulously researched the market, crafted a solid business model, and invested in top-notch marketing strategies. Confident in her preparation, she believed she completely controlled the situation. However, as the business grew, Kara realized that unforeseen challenges arose that she had not accounted for in her plans. Supply chain disruptions, unexpected competition, and fluctuating market trends tested her resilience and adaptability. Despite her best efforts to stay in control, Kara found herself overwhelmed by the rapidly changing business landscape.

Just as in the previous case study, Kara found herself amid unforeseen circumstances similar to Joe. Kara's Missing Variables were supply chain disruptions, unexpected competition, and fluctuating market trends. As she navigated through setbacks and uncertainties, Kara learned valuable lessons about flexibility and humility. She understood that being an entrepreneur meant embracing the unexpected and adapting quickly to new circumstances. With determination and a willingness to learn from her mistakes, Kara transformed moments of chaos into opportunities for growth and innovation. In the end, Kara discovered that while meticulous planning was essential, true success came from her ability to navigate the unpredictable nature of entrepreneurship with grace and resilience.

Flexibility and humility are valuable character qualities vital to a person's growth and business success. Flexibility allows you to adapt to changing circumstances and explore alternative solutions when faced with unexpected obstacles. By being open to new ideas and approaches, you can better pivot and adjust your plans to overcome challenges.

Humility plays a key role in navigating unexpected obstacles by allowing you to acknowledge your limitations and seek help when needed. It helps you approach situations with an open mind, learn from others, and accept feedback that can lead to better solutions. Together, flexibility and humility create a mindset that encourages resilience and growth in the face of unexpected obstacles. They enable you to remain agile, stay open to new possibilities, and maintain a positive attitude when confronted with challenges. Embracing these qualities can help you navigate uncertain situations with grace and adaptability, ultimately leading to more successful outcomes.

Determination and a willingness to learn are powerful attributes that can help navigate unexpected obstacles by providing a strong foundation for resilience and growth. When faced with challenges, determination fuels the drive to persevere and overcome difficulties, even when the path ahead seems uncertain. This resolute attitude can help maintain focus, motivation, and a positive mindset in the face of adversity. Moreover, a willingness to learn enables you to adapt, acquire new skills, and find creative solutions to unexpected obstacles.

Kevin had a chance to secure a major deal that could catapult his business to success. However, an unforeseen obstacle emerged in the form of a miscommunication that derailed the opportunity entirely. Frustrated and discouraged, he could have given up, but instead, he chose to learn from the mistake. With determination, Kevin reached out to the potential client to explain the situation and offer a sincere apology. Showing humility and a willingness to make things right, he not only salvaged the relationship but also gained respect for his honesty and integrity. Determined not to let such a setback happen again, Kevin dedicated himself to improving his communication skills and implementing better processes within his business. He sought mentorship and feedback from experienced professionals, eager to learn and grow from his mistakes. Eventually, Kevin's perseverance paid off. He not only secured the initial deal but went on to cultivate strong partnerships with other clients as well. Through his determination and willingness to learn from his mistakes, what seemed like a ruined opportunity transformed into a valuable lesson that propelled his business to new heights.

By approaching challenges with a growth mindset, you can embrace setbacks as opportunities for personal and business development and improvement. Learning from mistakes, seeking feedback, and exploring different perspectives can lead to innovative problem-solving strategies and a deeper understanding of the situation at hand. Ultimately, determination and a willingness to learn fosters resilience, adaptability, and a proactive approach to overcoming unexpected obstacles. Embracing these qualities can help you navigate uncertain circumstances with confidence, tenacity, and a sense of continuous growth and self-improvement. Incorporating determination, critical thinking, and flexibility into your business approach can enhance your problem-solving abilities, adapt to changes effectively, and make informed decisions that drive your business toward success.

Ways to incorporate more determination, critical thinking, and flexibility into your business sense:

1. *Set clear goals*: Define specific and achievable goals for your business that require determination to accomplish.

2. *Develop problem-solving skills*: Enhance your critical thinking abilities by actively seeking solutions to complex challenges that arise in your business operations.

3. *Embrace change*: Cultivate a flexible mindset open to new ideas, market trends, and customer feedback. Adapt quickly to changes in the business environment.

4. *Seek feedback*: Encourage a culture of feedback within your organization to gather different perspectives and insights that can help you make informed decisions.

5. *Take calculated risks*: Assess risks carefully and be willing to step out of your comfort zone to explore new growth opportunities.

6. *Continuously learn*: Invest in your professional development by seeking new knowledge, skills, and experiences to enhance your decision-making process.

7. *Surround yourself with diverse perspectives*: Engage with a diverse group of colleagues, mentors, other professionals, and advisors who can provide valuable insights and challenge your assumptions.

Developing appropriate character qualities such as resilience, adaptability, determination, humility, and awareness can help you remain strong and confident even when you are not in as much control as you thought. Resilience allows you to bounce back from setbacks and challenges, helping you to stay grounded and focused on moving forward. Adaptability enables you to adjust to changing circumstances and embrace uncertainty with an open mind, allowing you to navigate through unexpected situations confidently. Awareness helps you understand limitations and strengths and the circumstances surrounding you, enabling you to make informed decisions and maintain a sense of control over your actions and emotions. By cultivating these and other character traits, you can build inner strength and confidence that transcends external circumstances, empowering you to face uncertainties and challenges gracefully and resiliently.

Life is full of surprises, especially when it comes to business nuances. Unexpected events like job loss, medical emergencies, or natural disasters can throw even the best-laid plans off course. However, it's essential to remember that while you can't always control what happens to you, you can control how you respond. In times of work-related uncertainty, it's crucial to focus on what you can control. This includes approaching challenges positively, adapting to new situations, applying risk management methods, and seeking professional advice when needed.

By staying calm, flexible, and proactive, you can navigate through unexpected twists and turns with resilience and grace. Rather than dwelling on the unpredictability of life, you can use these moments as opportunities for growth and learning. Embracing change and facing challenges head-on can lead to personal and professional development, ultimately shaping you into a stronger and more capable person. So, the next time unexpected events come knocking at your door, remember to focus on what you can control and how you choose to respond. Your ability to adapt and overcome will not only help you weather the storm but also propel you toward success in the face of uncertainty.

Reflect:

1. Describe a work-related situation where an unexpected event overcame your perfect planning. Describe how this affected you. Describe how you felt. How did you respond? Journal your answers.

2. What have you learned about what you *cannot* control professionally despite your expertise as a result of this chapter? What have you learned about what you *can* control? How does this compare to your thoughts in the past? Journal your answers.

3. What part of the suggested resolutions do you find most challenging? How will you choose a more open-minded perspective? What can you do to ensure more stability in future outcomes? Journal your answers.

4. What are some dangers of not being prepared for unexpected business circumstances? What are some benefits of expecting the unexpected? Journal regarding the plans you will implement.

5. What are some benefits of a willingness to learn and adapt and determination in business decision-making? How can you improve your knowledge of this? Who is your accountability partner for venting when there is a "business blunder"? Journal the reasons you value this person.

6. Find ways to program determination, willingness to learn, flexibility, diversity, open-mindedness, and humility into your "preprogram." More information about how to "Reprogram Your Pre-Program" is found in *Elevate Your Mind to Success, Success Is Ele-MENTAL,* and at www.DrJillFandrich.com.

7. How will you utilize these skills to help other people? Journal your answers.

8. Who will you share this information with? Who will benefit most from it? Journal your answers.

9. Apply critical thinking to the information you learned. More about critical thinking is found in *Who Connects Your Dots?*, *Medically Speaking, Who Connects Your Dots?*, and *Students: Who Connects Your Dots?*

10. Practice the skills you learned daily. Journal and monitor your progress.

CHAPTER 14

Case Study Thirteen: Technical "Glitches"

Successful Forex trader Matt carefully prepared for what he believed would be an excellent trade. He has a history of high returns and quick executions. Matt analyzed market trends, indicators, and news, spending hours ensuring everything was in place for a profitable outcome. As he executed the trade, everything seemed to align perfectly. However, just as he anticipated reaping the rewards of his hard work, a sudden technological glitch struck. The trading platform froze at a crucial moment, preventing Matt from closing the trade at the optimal time. Despite his best efforts to resolve the issue quickly, precious seconds slipped away, and the market took an unexpected turn against him. Matt watched in disbelief as his carefully crafted trade crumbled before his eyes, leading to a substantial loss.

In the complex world of trading, every detail matters. The Missing Variable for Matt was the technical glitch that sent shockwaves through the market, causing chaos and confusion. It ultimately led to the failure of the trade. The unforeseen issue disrupted the trading process, causing significant financial repercussions and creating a chain reaction of negative consequences. This Missing Variable highlighted the importance of robust technical infrastructure and contingency plans in safeguarding against such incidents. In the aftermath of this event, it became clear that the technical glitch was the critical factor that ruined the trade, emphasizing the need for thorough risk assessment and mitigation strategies in complex trading environments. The lessons learned from this experience will undoubtedly shape future decisions and actions to prevent similar occurrences and protect against the impact of Missing Variables in the trading process.

Although devastated by the outcome, Matt remained resilient. He learned a valuable lesson about the unpredictable nature of technology in trading and the importance of being prepared for unforeseen challenges. Determined to bounce back, he embraced the setback as an opportunity to refine his strategies and enhance his risk management practices. Ultimately, Matt emerged stronger and more resourceful, using his experience to navigate future trades with caution and adaptability.

Risk management can help guard against technical glitches by identifying possible risks, assessing their potential impact, and implementing strategies to mitigate those risks. By conducting thorough risk assessments, you can proactively identify areas where technical glitches may occur and take steps to prevent or minimize their impact. Some ways risk management can help guard against technical glitches include implementing robust testing procedures to identify and address potential issues before they arise, regularly monitoring systems for anomalies or signs of impending failure, and developing contingency plans to quickly respond to and recover from technical glitches when they do occur. Additionally, risk management can help ensure that appropriate safeguards and controls are in place to protect against common technical issues such as data breaches, system failures, or cyber-attacks. By incorporating risk management practices into your operations, you can better anticipate, prevent, and respond to technical glitches, ultimately helping safeguard your systems and minimize disruption to your operations.

Enforcing risk management procedures can help businesses better prepare for unexpected technical glitches, enhance their resilience, and minimize the impact on operations and reputation.

Risk management steps:

1. *Identify and assess risks*: Conduct a thorough assessment to identify potential technical glitches that could impact the business operations.

2. *Develop a risk management plan*: Create a comprehensive plan outlining strategies to mitigate, transfer, or accept identified risks.

3. *Implement preventive measures*: Proactively address potential technical glitches by implementing preventive measures such as regular system updates, security patches, and disaster recovery plans.

4. *Train employees*: Provide training to employees on how to recognize and respond to technical glitches promptly to minimize potential disruptions.

5. *Regular monitoring and review*: Continuously monitor systems and processes to identify any emerging risks and update risk management procedures accordingly.

6. *Establish a response plan*: Develop a detailed response plan outlining the steps to be taken in the event of a technical glitch, including communication protocols and escalation procedures. Have a backup system in place, including a generator, to ensure function never ceases.

On an individual level, you can also be proactive in guarding against potential technical glitches. By following these proactive measures, you can minimize the impact of unforeseen glitches and ensure a smoother experience with your devices and systems.

Ways to be proactive against unforeseen technical glitches:

1. Regularly update software and applications to ensure they are running on the latest version with the latest security patches.

2. Back up important data regularly to prevent loss in the event of a technical glitch or system failure.

3. Install reliable antivirus software and perform regular scans to detect and remove any malware that could cause technical issues.

4. Educate yourself on common technical issues and troubleshooting techniques to be able to address them quickly if they arise.

5. Monitor system performance regularly for any signs of unusual behavior that could indicate a technical glitch.

6. Invest in quality hardware and equipment to reduce the likelihood of technical failures.

7. Create a contingency plan outlining steps to take in case of a technical glitch, including contacting technical support if needed.

8. Prepare a backup ethernet cord to ensure internet connectivity in case of wireless failure.

Planning for every possible obstacle is difficult due to the unpredictable nature of technology and the ever-evolving landscape of challenges that can arise. Technological advancements, system failures, cybersecurity threats, and unexpected changes can all disrupt even the most well-thought-out plans. Despite the difficulty, planning as comprehensively as possible when technology is involved is crucial. This proactive approach helps mitigate risks, minimize disruptions, and ensure smoother operations. By identifying potential obstacles and developing contingency plans, you can be better prepared to address challenges as they arise.

Tempy was a diligent project manager known for her proactive approach and meticulous planning. As the deadline for a critical business presentation approached, Tempy knew the importance of preparing for potential technical glitches that could hinder the success of the event. She made sure to have a backup laptop fully charged and ready to go, along with extra cables and adapters. Tempy also thoroughly tested the presentation equipment to ensure everything worked smoothly before the big day. During the presentation, just as she suspected, there was a minor technical glitch with the projector. Without missing a beat, she quickly switched to the backup laptop and continued the presentation seamlessly. Thanks to her proactive planning, the glitch was resolved within minutes, and the audience was impressed by Tempy's professionalism and preparedness. The event was a success, and the business received positive feedback from clients and stakeholders. Tempy's proactive approach and ability to plan ahead for technical glitches not only prevented complications but also demonstrated her reliability and dedication to ensuring the success of important business endeavors.

Planning for obstacles in advance allows for better resource allocation, improved decision-making, and increased resilience in the face of adversity. It helps you adapt to changes quickly and maintain a competitive edge in a fast-paced technological environment. While it may be impossible to anticipate every obstacle, putting effort into thorough planning can significantly enhance your ability to navigate challenges effectively and achieve your goals in the digital age.

In a digitally-driven world, ensuring a smooth online experience is vital. But what happens when unexpected internet issues strike, disrupting your connectivity? This uncertainty underscores the critical need for proactive planning to safeguard against such disruptions. From crucial business operations to personal communication, the impact of internet downtime can be profound. Imagine the frustration of a critical video conference being abruptly cut short due to connectivity issues or the stress of missing a deadline because of an unexpected outage. By anticipating and preparing for potential internet challenges, you can mitigate risks and maintain productivity in the face of adversity. Effective strategies like investing in backup internet solutions, creating contingency plans, and staying informed about service updates can make all the difference when the unexpected occurs. Embracing the importance of planning ahead for potential internet issues is not just prudent; it's essential for navigating the digital landscape with confidence and resilience. Prioritize preparedness to ensure that you can stay connected and productive, no matter what challenges may come your way.

Ways to plan ahead for potential internet issues:

1. *Redundant connections:* Have multiple internet service providers (ISPs) to switch to if one goes down. This could involve having both a wired and wireless connection.

2. *Backup equipment:* Keep spare modems, routers, and cables on hand in case of hardware failure.

3. *Cloud services:* Utilize cloud-based services so your data is still accessible even if your local network is down.

4. *Mobile hotspot*: Have a mobile hotspot or tethering option available as a backup internet source.

5. *Monitoring tools*: Use network monitoring tools to monitor your internet connection's performance and address any issues proactively.

6. *Emergency response plan*: Develop a clear plan of action for employees to follow in case of internet outages, including communication protocols and alternative work arrangements.

7. *Regular maintenance*: Stay proactive by regularly updating software, firmware, and security measures to prevent potential internet issues.

In a world of uncertainties and challenges, diligence is the compass that guides you through the storm. Like a vigilant sentinel, planning ahead becomes your armor against the unforeseen adversities lurking in the shadows. With careful foresight and unwavering determination, you pave the path toward success, one step at a time. Just as a skilled captain charts the course before setting sail, you, too, must anticipate the obstacles that may lie ahead. Through meticulous planning and strategic thinking, you fortify your defenses and stand resilient in the face of adversity. In the arena of life, it is not the swift nor the strong who prevail but the diligent and prepared who emerge victorious. So, heed the call to action and embrace the power of diligence and foresight. Rise above the challenges that seek to derail you with a steadfast resolve to conquer all that stands in your way, for it is in your diligence and meticulous planning that you find the strength to overcome any obstacle and the wisdom to navigate the turbulent waters of life with grace and resilience.

Diligence is a character quality that embodies perseverance, dedication, and hard work in all endeavors. Those who exhibit diligence show a strong commitment to their goals and tasks, working diligently and consistently to achieve success. They pay attention to every detail, striving for excellence in everything they do. Diligent people are focused, persistent, and self-disciplined, never giving up despite challenges or setbacks. Their unwavering dedication to their work often leads to impressive results and accomplishments. Diligence is a key trait in achieving your ambitions and fulfilling your potential. It is a quality that people across all walks of life highly value, as it demonstrates a strong work ethic and a willingness to put in the effort required to reach their objectives. In a world where hard work is often the key to success, diligence sets you apart and propels you toward your aspirations. By implementing certain strategies, you can cultivate a more diligent mindset and achieve your goals more effectively.

Ways to improve diligence:

1. *Set clear goals:* Define what you want to achieve and break it down into smaller, manageable tasks.

2. *Create a routine:* Establish a consistent schedule for work or study to build discipline and focus.

3. *Prioritize tasks:* Identify the most important tasks and work on those first to ensure progress on key objectives.

4. *Eliminate distractions:* Minimize interruptions and stay focused by turning off notifications and setting dedicated work hours.

5. *Stay organized:* Track deadlines, tasks, and progress to maintain a sense of control and direction.

6. *Develop good habits:* To increase productivity and efficiency, build positive habits, such as time management and goal setting.

7. *Stay educated:* Continuously learn and improve your skills in the field you are committed to. Read, listen to, and study as much information as possible to open your mind to new ideas, creativity, and innovation.

8. *Stay motivated:* Remind yourself of your goals and the reasons behind your work to maintain momentum and drive.

9. *Take breaks:* Allow yourself short breaks to recharge and prevent burnout, promoting sustained focus and productivity.

By incorporating specific strategies into your thinking process, you can enhance your strategic abilities and make more effective personal and professional decisions.

Ways to improve and apply strategic thinking:

1. *Develop a long-term vision*: Align your actions with long-term goals and objectives to stay focused on the big picture.

2. *Stay informed*: Continuously gather information about your industry, competitors, and market trends to make informed decisions.

3. *Think creatively*: Embrace creativity and think outside the box to develop innovative solutions to complex problems.

4. *Encourage collaboration*: Seek input from diverse perspectives within your team or organization to gain fresh insights and ideas.

5. *Prioritize and plan*: Use tools like SWOT (Strengths, Weaknesses, Opportunities, Threats) analysis, prioritization matrices, and action plans to organize your thoughts and strategies effectively.

6. *Adapt to change*: Be flexible and willing to adjust your strategies in response to changes in the internal or external environment.

7. *Reflect and learn*: Regularly review your decisions and outcomes to identify areas for improvement and learn from past experiences.

Combining risk management, diligence, and awareness is crucial for preparing for the unexpected. Risk management involves identifying potential threats and developing strategies to mitigate them. Diligence ensures thoroughness in planning and execution to minimize vulnerabilities. Awareness involves staying informed about current events and emerging risks to adapt strategies accordingly. Integrating these elements can enhance your preparedness for unexpected events. This approach enables the proactive identification of potential risks, implementation of effective mitigation measures, and prompt responses to emerging threats. Ultimately, combining risk management, diligence, strategic thinking, and awareness provides a comprehensive framework for building resilience and ensuring readiness in the face of uncertainty.

In a world where unexpected technical glitches are Missing Variables and can disrupt your plans in the blink of an eye, it's crucial to remember that not everything is within your control. By embracing a mindset that acknowledges the unpredictable nature of technology, you can better navigate these challenges with resilience and adaptability. So, next time a glitch throws a wrench in your plans, take a deep breath, assess what is within your control, and tackle the situation with a calm and focused mindset. Remember, in the face of uncertainty, your ability to adapt and problem-solve is your greatest asset.

 Reflect:

1. Recall a time when you were working on an important document on a computer, and it "froze" or shut down. How did this make you feel? How did you respond? What was the result of your response? Journal your answers.

2. What changes will you make to your technology as a result of this chapter? How often is technology an issue throughout your day or week? Journal your answers.

3. What challenges are involved with any of the suggested changes? How will you overcome them? What resources will you add to make this most effective? How can you improve your diligence? Journal your answers.

4. What are some dangers of not making any technological changes? What are some of the benefits of being proactive and making changes? Journal regarding the changes you will implement to minimize future technological issues.

5. Observe your current risk management practices. What seems to be effective? What doesn't seem to be working? Compare the

differences and journal your thoughts on the key differences. What do you notice? Journal your answers.

6. Find ways to program risk management strategies, SWOT analysis, diligence, strategic thinking, and awareness into your "preprogram." More information about how to "Reprogram Your Pre-Program" is found in *Elevate Your Mind to Success*, *Success Is Ele-MENTAL*, and at www.DrJillFandrich.com.

7. How will you utilize these skills in other areas of your life? Journal your answers.

8. Who will you share this information with? Who will benefit most from it? Journal your answers.

9. Apply critical thinking to the information you learned. More about critical thinking is found in *Who Connects Your Dots?*, *Medically Speaking, Who Connects Your Dots?*, and *Students: Who Connects Your Dots?*

10. Practice the skills you learned daily. Journal and monitor your progress.

CHAPTER 15

CONCLUSION

In the intricate tapestry of life, there will always be Missing Variables—unpredictable elements that challenge your sense of control. But remember, it's not about losing control; it's about how you navigate and respond to these unknowns that truly define your journey. Embrace the uncertainties, for they are the threads that weave resilience, adaptability, and growth into the fabric of your existence.

In the book *The Missing Variable*, we discussed many stories of situations where people responded and events that occurred with elements beyond control. Many variables we encounter in our lives throw an unexpected wrench into our best-laid plans. We discussed how people can provide unexpected responses or actions. We cannot control the actions, thoughts, responses, or decisions of other people—employees, bosses, spouses, friends, and even peer-pressure not-so-much-friends. Each person has his or her own free will and autonomy, which we must respect—or at least acknowledge. While we can influence and guide others through our words and actions, ultimately, people will make their own choices.

It is important to focus on what is within our control, such as our own thoughts, behaviors, and reactions. By letting go of the desire to control other people, we can cultivate healthier relationships and foster a greater sense of acceptance and understanding. Embracing this truth allows us to redirect our energy toward personal growth and self-improvement rather than being consumed by other people's actions. The only person we have full control over is ourselves.

We also discussed other Missing Variables, such as weather, traffic, and random unexplained circumstances. Just as with people, things occur that we have no control over, no matter how well we plan. Elements such as these occurrences remind us of life's unpredictability. Despite our best efforts to plan and prepare, these factors can often disrupt our routines and expectations. The weather can change in an instant, altering our plans and forcing us to adapt. Traffic jams can appear out of nowhere, causing delays and frustration. Unexplained circumstances, such as sudden road closures or unexpected health issues, can infuse a wrinkle in our carefully laid out schedules. It's a humbling reminder that there are forces beyond our control that influence our daily lives. The key lies in responding to these challenges with resilience and flexibility, accepting that not everything can be predicted or managed. Embracing the uncertainty and learning to navigate through these obstacles can ultimately lead to personal growth and a greater sense of adaptability in the face of life's inevitable curveballs.

We also considered the heartache of a single parent sharing a child through court-ordered visitations and struggles with rebellious teenagers. As a single parent navigating the complexities of sharing a child, the heartache can be profound. The struggles of dealing with teenagers navigating their own emotions, free will, and independence can add a layer of frustration and helplessness. These unexpected obstacles can feel overwhelming, leaving you feeling powerless in the face of circumstances beyond your control. Despite the challenges, resilience comes from facing adversity directly. The love for a child remains unwavering, serving as a guiding light through the darkest moments. Each setback is met with determination to overcome, knowing that the bond with a child is worth every struggle. Through the heartache and the struggles, you find strength in your role, knowing that your love and dedication will ultimately prevail. The journey may be fraught with obstacles, but the unwavering love for a child is a beacon of hope that sustains you through even the toughest of times.

Finally, we considered technological glitches and our lack of control over them. Technical glitches are inevitable in our modern digital world, often occurring without warning and beyond our control. Despite our best efforts to maintain stable systems, unpredictable errors can disrupt our daily routines and activities. These glitches can stem from various sources, such as software bugs, hardware malfunctions, or network issues, making them challenging to anticipate or prevent. In today's interconnected society, our reliance on technology makes us vulnerable to the impact of these unexpected disruptions. Whether it's a website crashing during peak hours, a device freezing at a critical moment, or a network outage causing delays, technical glitches can arise at any time and place. The frustration and inconvenience they cause serve as a reminder of the complex nature of our digital infrastructure and the limitations of our ability always to keep it running smoothly. As we navigate the digital landscape, it's crucial to recognize that technical glitches are a reality we must accept and adapt to. By maintaining a proactive mindset, staying informed about potential issues, and developing contingency plans and risk management procedures, we can better cope with these unforeseen challenges and minimize their impact on our daily lives.

One of the most challenging aspects of dealing with things beyond our control is accepting the uncertainty and unpredictability of the situation. It can be difficult for us to come to terms with the fact that some events, circumstances, or people are simply "out of our hands," no matter how much we wish otherwise. This lack of control can lead to feelings of frustration, anxiety, and helplessness, which can be mentally and emotionally taxing. Not being able to influence or change certain outcomes can challenge our sense of agency and volition, potentially impacting our self-esteem and confidence. The inability to control external factors may also trigger feelings of vulnerability and insecurity, forcing us to confront our limitations and surrender to the unknown.

Despite these challenges, developing resilience, adaptability, security, and a mindset focused on what *can* be controlled rather than what cannot help us navigate situations beyond our control more effectively. Embracing uncertainty as a natural part of life and focusing on personal growth and learning can also aid in coping with the challenges posed by uncontrollable circumstances.

In a world where variables constantly shift and unexpected changes leave us feeling lost, one thing remains certain: our ability to adapt and grow. When faced with missing pieces in our lives, it's easy to succumb to feelings of confusion and helplessness. But what if we shift our perspective? Instead of fixating on what we lack, we can embrace the uncertainty as an opportunity for self-discovery, resourcefulness, innovation, and resilience. By acknowledging that we cannot control every aspect of our lives, we open ourselves up to new possibilities and growth. It is in these moments of vulnerability that we can truly understand our strength and capacity for adaptation.

So, when faced with Missing Variables, choose to respond with courage and an open mind. Courage isn't the opposite of fear. Rather, it is knowing things aren't as expected, yet facing them head-on with determination and a positive mindset anyway. Embrace the unknown as a chance to define your own narrative and create a future that is uniquely yours. Remember, it is not the missing pieces that define us but how we *choose to respond* despite them. Fill the voids with courage and grace. Surrender to the flow of the river rather than trying to swim against it!

Reflect:

1. What is the most memorable point you will take away from this book? What makes it most memorable? Journal your answers.

2. How will you apply this to your life? How many of the Missing Variables have you experienced? Describe a few of them. How have your responses changed for responding to unexpected circumstances? Journal your answers.

3. What is the biggest challenge involved with suggestions made? How will you overcome it? What resources will you utilize to make this most effective? Establish steps to overcome this challenge. Journal your answers.

4. Rewrite your goals and update them either daily or weekly.

5. What are some benefits of being proactive with changes? Journal regarding the changes you will implement to minimize future issues.

6. What is your biggest concern about Missing Variables? Which category of Missing Variables do you encounter the most? How have your responses changed? Journal your answers.

7. What other qualities, skills, or strategies will you "Reprogram in Your Pre-Program"? For more information, refer to *Elevate Your Mind to Success*, *Success Is Ele-MENTAL*, and www. DrJillFandrich.com.

8. How will you utilize this information in your life? Journal your answers.

9. Who will you share this book with? Who comes to mind that will benefit most from it? Journal your answers.

10. Apply critical thinking to the information you learned. More about critical thinking is found in *Who Connects Your Dots?*, *Medically Speaking, Who Connects Your Dots?*, and *Students: Who Connects Your Dots?*

11. Practice the skills you learned daily. Journal and monitor your progress.

JOURNAL

Great thinkers are note-worthy.

—Jill Fandrich

Date:
Topic:

What is the identified Missing Variable? What can't I control?

What is the desired outcome? What actually occurred?

What mistakes did I make?

How can I do it differently next time? What can I control?

What did I do right?

What have I learned from this experience?

Other questions:

JOURNAL

Great thinkers are note-worthy.

—Jill Fandrich

Date:
Topic:

What is the identified Missing Variable? What can't I control?

What is the desired outcome? What actually occurred?

What mistakes did I make?

How can I do it differently next time? What can I control?

What did I do right?

What have I learned from this experience?

Other questions:

JOURNAL

Great thinkers are note-worthy.

—Jill Fandrich

Date:
Topic:

What is the identified Missing Variable? What can't I control?

What is the desired outcome? What actually occurred?

What mistakes did I make?

How can I do it differently next time? What can I control?

What did I do right?

What have I learned from this experience?

Other questions:

JOURNAL

Great thinkers are note-worthy.

—Jill Fandrich

Date:
Topic:

What is the identified Missing Variable? What can't I control?

What is the desired outcome? What actually occurred?

What mistakes did I make?

How can I do it differently next time? What can I control?

What did I do right?

What have I learned from this experience?

Other questions:

JOURNAL

Great thinkers are note-worthy.

—Jill Fandrich

Date:
Topic:

What is the identified Missing Variable? What can't I control?

What is the desired outcome? What actually occurred?

What mistakes did I make?

How can I do it differently next time? What can I control?

What did I do right?

What have I learned from this experience?

Other questions:

JOURNAL

Great thinkers are note-worthy.

—Jill Fandrich

Date:
Topic:

What is the identified Missing Variable? What can't I control?

What is the desired outcome? What actually occurred?

What mistakes did I make?

How can I do it differently next time? What can I control?

What did I do right?

What have I learned from this experience?

Other questions:

JOURNAL

Great thinkers are note-worthy.

—Jill Fandrich

Date:
Topic:

What is the identified Missing Variable? What can't I control?

What is the desired outcome? What actually occurred?

What mistakes did I make?

How can I do it differently next time? What can I control?

What did I do right?

What have I learned from this experience?

Other questions:

Printed in the USA
CPSIA information can be obtained
at www.ICGtesting.com
CBHW030134041024
15319CB00043B/393